Failure of European Multiculturalism

The Islamist Crusade

By
GENNARO BUONOCORE
and
CHRISTIAN VON ROSEN-KREUTZ

Failure of European Multiculturalism: The Islamist Crusade
Copyright © 2012 by Jackson Hill Press

For information about this title or to order other books and/or electronic media, contact the publisher:
Jackson Hill Press
Rancho Santa Margarita, California
www.jacksonhillpress.com
(949) 533-4050

ISBN: 978-0-9855762-0-2

Terrorism, Extremist, European Multi-Culturalism

Printed in the United States of America

Cover and Interior design by: 1106 Design

Acknowledgments

Si risolve ben poco con la mitraglia e col nerbo.
L'ipotesi che tutto sia un bisticcio,
uno scambio di sillabe è la più attendibile.
Non per nulla in principio era il Verbo.

Very little is solved with the use of a
machine gun or a whip
A verbal misunderstanding is the most
probable cause of a conflict.
This is why at the beginning was the Word.
— EUGENIO MONTALE

THIS BOOK IS NOT MEANT to be a call to arms; it is not meant to resemble the appeal from Byzantine Emperor Alexios I Komenos to Pope Urban II, which effectively started the First Crusade. The book is not a condemnation of *Islamism* or Islamic fundamentalism. As a born and raised Christian I see the attraction in the purity of Saudi *Wahhabism*, especially when it is not intended as a declaration of war on Western lifestyle. I can even see the appeal of the monastic choice of a *Salafi* whose Spartan approach to existence seeks to counter the greed and valueless onslaught of perceived modernity. What this book is about is the inherent failure generated by the willingness to accept others and their uniqueness.

This book is not a study on domestic-bred terrorism. Whether some European mosques teach intolerance to their *madafa* pupils to the point of instigating mass murder is a matter of study for enforcement agencies no less than is clamping down on neo-Nazist resurgence or other forms of European ultra-nationalism.

The book should be a warning shot to signal that a forced approach to multiculturalism has failed to address the fundamental differences that make societies thrive in their uniqueness.

At times the narrative might sound radical and intransigent but the hard tones are only meant to spark a much-needed reflection and a constructive engagement. The narrative is also a compendium of the opinion of many experts, scholars and journalists as reported widely on the web and through readily available publications.

The harshness of some of our statements is meant to dispel apathy and promote social participation. There is no substitute for dialogue even when it involves tough words.

The accuracy of this study would not have been possible without the creative support and painstaking research of a long-standing associate of mine who, for the purpose of his desire for anonymity, I will call Christian Von Rosen-Kreutz.

To my friend, who best describes the essence of the learned *Mitteleuropean* goes all my gratitude and recognition for analyzing the troublesome patterns that are developing in modern Europe. Within twelve months of accurate research, scouting countless website pages and reading accurate literature, he was able to assemble a collage of accurate statements and excerpts from studies of sector experts and accomplished writers and journalists. This book makes ample reference to the learned statements of these individuals and organizations and seeks support in its findings by quoting them in the appropriate context. Reading this book is like going through a digest, a compendium, of the relevant opinions of many opinion makers. The reason for quoting and using a large amount of different opinions, who seem to come to rest on the same conclusions, is to highlight the deep concerns that are shared by many people.

The timing of the book's publishing has proved a challenge as the writing has become a constant work in progress that has required numerous updates because of the ever-changing geo-political scenario in the Mediterranean basin. By the time the first draft was completed, our forecast of political changes in Egypt had proven a reality.

To my publisher, Jackson Hill Press, go my thanks for believing that this work was interesting enough to be made available to the general public and most importantly for their patience in understanding the nuances and literary liberties that European academics take for granted but have no equivalent in the American world.

To the editor, graphic designer and all others who have made the distribution of this book possible go my most sincere appreciation for their well-done job and their professional attitude.

Salaam aleikum,
Gennaro Buonocore

Failure of European Multiculturalism
The Islamist Crusade

Immigration?
What immigration?

"We have 50 million Muslims in Europe. There are
signs that Allah will grant Islam victory in Europe—
without swords, without guns, without conquests.
The 50 million Muslims of Europe will turn it into
a Muslim continent within a few decades."[1]

— MUAMMAR AL-QADHAFI

FOLLOWING THE SEVENTH-CENTURY Muslim military offensives against Byzantium, European powers instinctively and militarily resisted Jihad—when necessary—for over a millennium to protect their independence. However, the response in the late twentieth century has become drastically different; Europe, as reflected by the confused and cautious response by the institutions of the European Union, has abandoned resistance embracing an approach of passive tolerance seeking full integration of Islamic and other cultures such as the *Indochinese*. The beginning of the millennium saw a subtle but certain shifting of cultural values towards a different and relatively less familiar form of social structure. Europeans began perceiving their land as becoming a multicultural

---

[1]   Libyan leader Muammar al-Qadhafi, in a speech that aired on Al-Jazeera TV on April 10, 2006

1

patchwork, not a USA-styled "melting pot" but a disjointed collection of cultural realities—entire neighborhoods were changing, the old citizens were moving out and new citizens took over the space left unchartered, leading to new habits, new odors and new faces. Taking a stroll around the popular Piazza Vittorio in downtown Rome is one of the most striking pictures of how *Umbertine* style architecture can house Middle Eastern bazaars and Mandarin shi'chang.

But in reality, the need for integration weakened the traditional structure of European values; old customs were challenged and moral relativism gained ground amongst the younger generations. In the new Europe anything coexisted with its opposite. The golden rule was to keep all changes under control. Evidently this change in the social fabric generated uneasiness and psychological distress among people, which was reflected in a constant increase in delinquency (up by 20% in urban areas between 2003 and 2009) and the increase of medical expenditures for psychotropic drugs (an increase of 35% between 2002 and 2008).[2] Another consequence of this social instability was the sudden shift of the electorate to the right—or even extreme right—wing political parties across Europe—political analysts reckon about a doubling of the conservative and right wing votes over the five years between 2005 and 2010.[3] Nonetheless, despite popular disapproval, the European States' approaches to immigration were not substantially altered until 2003 and then again in 2010, when the situation was already heavily compromised. During these years of denial, European governments knowingly

---

[2]   The 2010 World Drug report, World Health Organization, Geneva, See: http://www.unodc.org/unodc/en/data-and-analysis/WDR-2010.html

[3]   Parlemeter—February 2011, European Parliament Eurobarometer (EB Parlemeter 74.3), See: http://ec.europa.eu/public_opinion/archives/ebs/ebs_parl_74-3_synth_en.pdf

refused to confront the social impact of immigration, replacing proper policy with a virtual world of rhetoric that replaced reality. In fact the post–Judeo-Christian European attitude is better described as "dhimmitude",[4] which, according to the Egyptian-born British writer and political commentator Gisèle Orebi—better known as Bat Ye'or—is the legal and social condition of non-Muslims subjected to Islamic rule. The word "dhimmitude" comes from dhimmi, an Arabic word meaning "protected." Dhimmi was the label given by Arab-Muslim conquerors "to indigenous non-Muslim populations who surrendered by a treaty (dhimma) to Muslim domination and to laws based on the Shari'a."[5] There are many indicators of this fundamental attitude in European policy, suffice to mention a couple that are more evident, namely "anti-Americanism, anti-Semitism and 'Palestinization.'"[6,7] With the recrudescence of Palestinian terrorist Jihad, European Foreign Affairs Commissioner Chris Patten declared to the European Parliament, on January 31, 2001, that "Europe's foreign policy should give special attention to its southern flank" (the Arab countries, in EU jargon), adding that he was "delighted by the general agreement to give greater visibility to the Mediterranean Partnership."[8] With respect to the United States, Europe, Israel and Arab countries, Euro-Arab Dialogue determines complex policies and comprises many different aspects. A global Pan-Islamic movement is currently

---

[4]   Dhimmitude is the Islamic system of governing populations conquered by Jihad wars, encompassing all of the demographic, ethnic and religious aspects of the political system.—From Wikipedia, the free encyclopedia

[5]   "Islam and the *Dhimmis:* Rejoinder," *The Jerusalem Quarterly* (1987):42, pp. 83–88

[6]   Ibid.

[7]   By Palestinization, we refer to all freedom movements of the people of Magreb and Mashreq, notably the uprisings against so-called oppressive governments of the Arab Spring of 2011.

[8]   Cris Patten at the European Parliament, January 2001, See: http://eeas.europa.eu/news/patten/sp01_49.htm

transforming Europe into a new continent of "dhimmitude" within a worldwide strategy of Jihad and da'wa, the latter being the pacific method of Islamization. The full extent of this policy of dhimmitude for the Euro-Arabian continent is analyzed and expressed in the "Rapport du Comité des Sages" that was submitted to European Commission president Romano Prodi in October 2003.[9] This policy piece, entitled "Dialogue between Peoples and Cultures in the Euro-Mediterranean Region," was accepted by the European Union in December 2003. Notwithstanding its objectives, not only has this Dialogue not generated a better climate of acceptance and respect across of the Mediterranean, but it has not prevented or even flagged the upcoming popular revolts that shook the Maghreb and Mashreq regions with— euphemistically speaking—uncertain democratic outcomes. Europe was taken abreast when Tunisia and Egypt overthrew their government and even worse when Syria and Libya massacred its people in the spring of 2011. Nobody expected it, but it happened. The ruthlessness and violence shown by the Arab governments against its own citizens make us wonder how they would behave against foreign or simply diverging views. A possible preview is shown in Egypt where 8 million Christian Copts are struggling to survive in a country swept by a democratic and freedom movement named the Arab Spring. If democratically elected Muslim governments of the Maghreb and Mashreq refuse to apply tolerance and democracy with its people, how can the international community expect Muslims in Europe to be following a process of Western democratization? Rather, the more the West becomes compliant to accommodate the religious and political norms of Muslim immigrants out of a fear of social unrest and

---

[9]   See: http://ec.europa.eu/culture/documents/publications/dialogue_fr.pdf

terrorism, the more Islam becomes bold and extreme in its claims for cultural predominance. These increasingly visible aspects of European policy in the early part of the decade are merely components of a greater overall "transformation of Europe into a new geopolitical entity, namely Eurabia."[10]

There are plenty of references and analyses about the Eurabia concept springing up in European journalism and politics at present. To understand the process of "Eurabization," it is important to understand the historic perspective; Islam never lived the Enlightenment nor the Marxist struggle for civil and economic rights. In fact, through history, Islam only willingly accepted the laws that accept, or at least do not contradict, the precepts of the Sharia. The well-established and respected Sheikh Abdurraheem Green, formerly British citizen Anthony Green, in his speeches on Islam and democracy[11] convincingly explained how democracy and Islam are mutually exclusive, for "When one of the systems rules the other cannot coexist." With political, economic, religious, cultural and media components, Eurabia designates a new entity superimposed on Europe by powerful governmental lobbies.[12] While Europeans live within Eurabia's constraints, beyond a somewhat confused awareness, few are really conscious of them on a daily basis. Eurabia is the agents and enforcers of this all-encompassing new Eurabic policy and culture. The tension perceived and the sense of misplacement arises from fundamental and uncompromising differences over societal, political and cultural values, as well as core religious identities. Europe's cultural identity is defined by

---

[10]   Bat Ye'or, "Le dialogue Euro-Arabe et la naissance d'Eurabia," Observatoire du monde juif 4/5 (December 2002)

[11]   See: http://www.deen-ul-islam.org/islam-democracy-abdurraheem-green

[12]   Bat Ye'or, "Le dialogue Euro-Arabe et la naissance d'Eurabia," Observatoire du monde juif 4/5 (December 2002)

a clear sense of place, a sense of history and a sense of self; it evolved from Hellenic and Judeo-Christian roots. Being European rests on the founding principles inherited from the Enlightenment period: individual liberty and equality before the law and freedom of religious belief. The vibrant economy and the flourishing society of Europe built on the ambition of its people, their shared values and vision of the future: all this is trembling and is at serious peril.

Finally, it is important to remember that, at the current rates of demographic growth, European native white Caucasians are set to become a minority in 2060. By that time, Muslims will account for about thirty-five percent of the total population, mostly young and more prolific than non-Muslim Europeans. This large minority will have voting rights. Will they politically choose the right, the left or Muslim? If the latter prevails, the birth of Eurabia and the extinction of Europe as we know it—with its culture, heritage and identity—might well be a *fait accompli.*

European history has not been a traditional example of separation between church and state, especially in Mediterranean nations such Italy and Spain, but the mild approach of the Roman Catholic Church of the past century cannot be compared with the politics of religious movements like the Egyptian Muslim Brotherhood or the Lebanese Hizbollah. Even including the *Opus Dei,* there is simply no equivalent religious movement in Europe with the same *pressure* capacity that Islamic movements have on their domestic governments.

Why talk about this now? There has never been a better time in European history to address the social difficulties that are contributing to the impending collapse of the European financial system and its political structure. Discussing this scenario as early as 2009 would have helped classify this analysis as the typical sci-fi depiction of an apocalyptic world. Doing it at the end of 2011, with the world witnessing a meltdown of Europe as we knew it, brings the issue closer to home, a more acceptable reality, which needs to be assessed in its full cause.

The financial crisis that has hit the continent signaled an end of the fiscal resources that most European states require in order to fund social and assistance initiatives. Most of these countries with limited natural resources and a diminishing competitiveness of their industrial sectors are facing catastrophic public debt that can only be serviced by a GDP growth that is impossible to achieve.

The demographic changes that are increasing pressure on these social and assistance initiatives in a scenario of low GDP growth rate and rising unemployment are the fuse that will most likely detonate the civilian disturbance bomb.

Conflicts experienced in the countries that recently saw the Arab Spring will then extend to neighboring Europe with some of the original Arab protagonists playing a major part in them. This scenario is the reality of the next five years.

If Europe has failed in its promise to be a viable alternative to the American cohesive societal reality then let's analyze what were the causes and what some of the solutions might be.

How did we get here?

I consider it part of my responsibility as President
of the United States to fight against negative
stereotypes of Islam wherever they appear.
— BARACK OBAMA[13]

THREATENED BY IMMIGRATION and failed multiculturalism, lacking a coordinated policy to enhance integration by the unwilling, crumbling on its ethical and moral values, dragged in an expensive war against terror that cannot be won, Europe's very existence is at stake. In absence of urgent political initiatives, the original Europeans will be reduced to a silent minority within a maximum of three generations—demographics and immigration rates show it is only a matter of when—not if—it will happen.

A significant role in the population dynamics and population composition of European societies is played by migration. Therefore, the study of demographical composition and the segmentation of the foreign and foreign-born population is crucial to understanding how the EU population is evolving. The total number of non-nationals living on the territory of the EU Member States, as of January 1, 2008, was 40.51 million,

---

[13] Remarks of Barack Obama in the Grand Hall of Cairo University on June 4, 2009. See full text: http://www.time.com/time/politics/article/0,8599,1902738,00.html

representing 8.3% of the population.[14] The trend is increasing as more than one-third of the non-nationals (14.9 million) were previously residents of another EU Member State. Separately revealed by a detailed analysis of the current age structure of nationals and non-nationals is that non-nationals bring a younger population to the EU. In absolute terms, the largest numbers of foreign citizens reside in Germany, Spain, the United Kingdom, France and Italy. In these five countries, non-nationals represent more than 75% of the total EU foreign population. In relative terms, Luxembourg is the EU Member State with the highest share of foreigners, where foreigners make up 43.5% of the usually resident population. In 2009, a high proportion of non-nationals (10% or more of the resident population) was also recorded in Latvia, Estonia, Cyprus, Spain, Ireland and Austria, as well as in one of the EFTA [European Fair Trade Association] countries, Switzerland.[15]

The outlook for the coming decades shows an interesting growth trend. Immigrants tend to be younger than the European native population average and are mostly in reproductive age. The average immigrant family counts 2.5 children, across all Europe; this rate ranges from Asian (2.2) to Caucasian non-EU (1.5) and to African (2.8), however the average Muslim couple across all European regions reaches 3.9 children. In the public primary school system, non-natives account from 8 to 25% of all pupils as it varies across different regions in Europe. In 2005, the UK Office of National Statistics (ONS) issued a separate report that stated that 36% of all births in England and Wales were not "white

---

[14]   Migrants to Work, Innovative approaches towards successful integration of third country migrants into the labour market. This study has been financed by European Commission, B. Frouws, MSc, Drs. B.J. Buiskool, Zoetermeer, March 4, 2010, pg. 41

[15]   Eurostat Statistics Focus, 45/2010, Sept. 2010

European."[16] The 2005 birth rate figure does not include births to second- and third-generation immigrant families who still retain a strong national identity from their original countries. Figures released by the UK's ONS in January 2010 revealed that the immigrant Muslim population in Europe had grown by more than 6.8 million to 26.4 million in just four years. Due to migratory relocation and *non-naturalized* births, the Muslim population is predicted to double in 10 years, a stunning growth rate if analyzed in a context of zero overall growth of the native European population.

Therefore, supported by statistical evidence from different non-partisan sources, there is a clear indication that ethnicities originating in immigration will overwhelm the original population of Europe within the next 40 years. In other words, so-defined native Europeans may be a minority by 2050.

It is a fact that the admission of large numbers of foreigners into Europe has, over the past decade, created a less affluent, more violent, less productive, confused, ill-educated, fractured society, notably in urban areas. Immigration in Western Europe—including those countries that until a decade or two ago registered negative net migration—is approaching levels "seen in North America on the eve of the First World War—the peak of migration to the new world. In Ireland today, for example, the share of the foreign-born among the population is 11.3%, compared with 14.7% in the United States in 1910."[17] Conversely, since the late '60s immigration policy in Western Europe was characterized by a deeply rooted and subtle guilt complex coming from

---

[16]   Birth weight and gestational age by ethnic group, England and Wales 2005: introducing new data on births, Kath Moser, Office for National Statistics
[17]   Yesterday's policies, today's problems, by Toby Vogel, The European Voice, March 31, 2011

anti-colonialist remorse and euro-socialist polity permeated by a whim for social revenge for the benefit of people's revolutions and liberal reforms across the third world. This liberal approach opened the door to masses of labor immigrants to enter and settle, with little restrictions, in the social landscape of Western and Eastern Europe. In a way, the easy immigration was fueled by the strong economic growth experienced in the European countries and the immigrant was perceived as a fellow worker—a comrade—by the blue-collar social classes, the proletarian workforce in need of additional muscle and capacity. It was also welcome by the European white-collar segment that saw a chance for cheaper cost of labor and an increase in low paid services that the native Europeans were unwilling to perform. Urban studies professor Paul Scheffer of the University of Amsterdam describes the "impact of rapid, large-scale immigration on urban neighborhoods (such as Brussels' Molenbeek-Saint-Jean or Berlin's Neukölln) and the social tensions generated by the clash of old and new ways of life. His observation of the enabling role that modern technology, from satellite TV to Skype, plays in perpetuating parochial, rural lifestyles rings very true."[18] What emerges from this account is that today's challenges are the product of yesterday's policies. Millions of low-skilled Italians, Moroccans, Yugoslavs and Turks were brought to Western Europe to work in mines, on construction sites or in factories. Contrary to expectations, they stayed, and international rules on family reunification allowed their spouses, children and parents to join them. These migrants became residents, and quite often citizens. "In half of Amsterdam's primary schools today, the children of low-skilled immigrants from outside Europe make up 70%

---

[18]   Ibid.

or more of the student body."[19] Prof. Scheffer insists that the US and Western Europe are "more similar on many issues related with migration than they might appear. Ethnic segregation in cities, for example, is at comparable levels, if we leave aside the extreme segregation of the African-American population."[20] Contrary to the religious growth trends in the United States, Islam has become a major Western European cult not only because around 40 million Muslims are now thought to live in Europe, but mainly because many of them hold religious views that are obtruded onto the local population.[21] When the economic crisis hit in the mid-seventies, immigration flows became better regulated and dropped dramatically by the early '80s. By the time a number of European countries had large immigrant communities, primarily the UK, France, Germany and Sweden, i.e., the more industrialized areas. As unemployment grew, the immigrant workers were economically motivated to return to their countries of origin, however only a limited number elected to. In fact, their countries of origin were also experiencing economic recession or were feeling the lack of freedom dictated by non-democratic ruling. The military coup in Turkey in 1980, for instance, discouraged a number of Turkish unemployed workers to return to a much cheaper and more welcoming lifestyle. Faced with more pressing social and economic needs, European governments focused on saving the declining industrial sectors and controlling the growing domestic unease before it hit upheaval. Labor and employment issues became priority on the political agendas and in the election campaigns across the continent. Twenty years later those priorities are even

---

[19] Ibid.
[20] Ibid.
[21] Immigrant Nations, Paul Scheffer, Polity Press, May 2011

more dire. Higher unemployment had a direct impact on the political choice of the voting electorate. Because of the chosen social policies, immigration and asylum regulations, as well as the entering in the EU of up to 1 million illegal immigrants each year became taboos that could never be spoken about. Less than half of all illegal immigrants are still today identified and repatriated—a significant part of these individuals show up on the enforcement agencies, radars because of misdemeanors or more serious offenses. This continues to be a highly controversial and politically incorrect issue that leads to social malaises, such as delinquency (crime), that most traditional political parties have chosen not to discuss publicly or denied it even existed. However, there is little denying that the immigration emergency is increasingly serious and is finally influencing any politician's district. Quite apart from the enormous costs, which are estimated at several billion Euros per year, problems have arisen across the continent that include: social breakdowns, the deterioration of a cohesive community spirit and neighborliness, the erosion of heritage and cultural history, the promulgation of legislation alien to the native constituency, the erosion of the countryside in favor of urban monstrosities with a correspondent pressure on social services and the birth of *de facto* ghettos that have replaced the picturesque villages that constituted the pretty picture of traditional European suburbia.

Immigration is not an easy social dynamic to deal with, especially in the short term. Ideally it should take time to plan and it should to be carried out progressively. Not all immigrants have the same ability and versatility to adapt to a new cultural environment. Socio-cultural distance from the host nation plays an important role in the assimilation process. There are cultures that are used to migration and have a faster and more natural approach to integration. Other cultures are more difficult to assimilate but eventually, through the opportune induction and joint education, become integrating parts of the host country. Finally, there are some cultures that are resilient to assimilation and integration; some of these cultures may have periods of greater or lesser penetration into the new surrounding social environments, but in most cases interaction with other peoples is dictated by a slow process whereby mutual trust is difficult to achieve and the old beliefs are hardly replaced by the new. These are cultures that reject integration and preserve their national salient traits through the domination of surrounding space and by overriding the host nation's existing traditions. These cultures are invasive, aggressive but also inclusive. Proselytism and expansion is part of their historical makeup. These few cultures see their migration as an opportunity to broaden their base and grow by achieving domestic social stability. The most widely spread culture of this kind is the Islamic.

Islam has been growing in depth and width in most parts of the world. Since the late eighties, Europe has become a favorite shore for Islamic immigration, especially from the neighboring African and Asian countries. Such preference is primarily due to its geographical proximity, attractive wealth and very socialist labor and legislation. It is now undisputed that liberal parties as well as the socialist group at the European Parliament deliberately engineered mass immigration over the last 30 years. Recent revelations from Labor Party officials in the UK have confirmed that immigration has been orchestrated and deliberately employed to dilute European political connotation and to manipulate the EU electoral system. "Former Labor advisor Andrew Neather admitted that the social objective of Labor's immigration policy was to rub the Right's nose in diversity and render their arguments out of date."[22] Since the seventies, liberal and left wing parties across Europe introduced a deliberate policy of undermining European socio-political identity—notably traditional, conservative and centered on Christian-democratic belief. The plan has brought a vast majority of European citizens to challenge traditional values and religious beliefs, making them easy prey of materialism and cynical nihilism. Promoting a lack of fundamental stabilizing values and depriving society of the liberal conservative bedrock created the void on which multiculturalism and other forms of belligerent religious recruitment have thrived. Flags, national anthems and shows of military prowess are a double-edged sword and Europeans are wary of their ultra-nationalist use that brought the tragedy of two world wars, but these symbols also possess that benefit of integrating society under a common identity that transcends mere individualism and seconds personal interests to the benefit of society at large. Condemning the use and promotion of these symbols became a useful mocking tool to criticize political parties or factions defined as neo-fascist or racist in their bias. Also, European citizenship was given away as a natural right rather than a privilege based on merit. A number of Al Qaida operatives have pursued attacks on European targets while holding citizenships of EU member nations. The EU institutions have, therefore, an obligation to urgently review their bilateral and multilateral naturalization agreements (made since the early '70s), to ensure that the honor and the benefit of European citizenship is awarded to people who are willing to contribute to the host continent society (and world society at large)

---

[22] How Labour threw open doors to mass migration in secret plot to make a multicultural UK By James Slack, daily mail online, February 10, 2010

and its well-being. Citizenship should be closely linked to employment opportunities and moral character. Employment confers dignity and when immigrants hold a job, they can feel dignified as contributing members of their community and can resist the temptation of delinquency or illegal shortcuts.

In the past few years, the deadly combination of migratory flows, technology advances and economic downturns have caused a net decrease in job opportunities across Europe. Employment figures released by Eurostat show that the EU-27 employment rate for individuals aged 15 to 64 decreased in 2009 to 64.6%, down from 65.9% in 2008. Conversely, Eurostat estimated that 23.048 million men and women in the EU-27 were unemployed in January 2011. Compared with January 2007, the unemployment figure rose by 5 million individuals. The Euro area's seasonally adjusted unemployment rate was 10% in January 2011; it was 9.5% in January 2010. Statistics from 2011 indicate that, among the EU countries, the highest rates are in Spain (20.4%), Latvia (18.3%) and Lithuania (17.4%).

The millions of migrants have now become a source of social distress. Their loyalty and adherence to Western values is questionable, notably when holding double citizenship as identified in the study of thousands of northern African immigrants. Is an individual, who holds both Tunisian and French citizenships, Tunisian or French first? Is he French or Muslim first? In the US, despite traditionally strong communities such as the Irish, Italian and Hispanic ones, most citizens have passed the test of full integration when a lot of these people have given their life on battlefields across the world side by side. European armies and police forces have very little request of enrollment coming from Islamic communities. Ironic, considering the military has traditionally been the go to employer for financially strapped social classes. Isn't this a clear sign that European cohesiveness is indeed at stake? "Some have questioned whether allowing dual citizenship impedes cultural assimilation, increases 'disconnectedness' from the political process, and degrades national identity/cohesiveness."[23] The rise in tension between host nation and migrant communities is often mentioned as evidence of the need to maintain a strongly unifying national identity and culture. It is safe to assert that "...the fact that a second citizenship, for example the European passport, can be obtained without giving anything up (e.g., the loss of public benefits, welfare, healthcare, retirement funds, and job opportunities in the country of origin in exchange for citizenship in a new country) both trivializes what it means to be a citizen"[24] and "...nullifies the consequential, transformational, and psychological change that occurs in an individual when they go through the naturalization process."[25] A study carried out by the University of Bielefeld in 2008 shows that holding dual citizenship can actually promote embracing political activity that provides "an avenue for immigrants who are unwilling to forsake their country of origin either out of loyalty or due to a feeling of separation from the mainstream society because of language, culture, religion, or ethnicity."[26]

In the United States, the concern over the effect of multiple citizenship on national cohesion is generally more acute. There seem to be two main reasons to this concern—the first one is that the United States is not an "ethnic" nation, but a

---

[23]   Staton, Jeffrey K. (Florida State University); Jackson, Robert A. (Florida State University); Camache, Damaryas (University of Illinois): "Dual Nationality Among Latinos: What are the Implications for Political Connectedness"
[24]   Renshon, Stanley: "Dual Citizenship and American National Identity," Center for Immigration Studies, 2001
[25]   Ibid.
[26]   Faist, Thomas; Gerdes, Jurgen (Bielefeld University): "Dual Citizenship in an Age of Mobility," 2008

"civic" nation. For many, the coveted American citizenship is based on loyalty and allegiance to American democratic institutions and values. Naturalizing as a US citizen is not achieved by belonging to a particular ethnicity. The second reason is that due to its generous immigration policy of taking in and absorbing a very diverse array of immigrants, the United States has prospered as an immigrant nation.

In other words, it is clear that the degree of scrutiny over the effects of dual citizenship seemingly defines a country's model for properly managing integration in the context of immigration and ethnic diversity.

In Europe, immigrants have historically been accepted as temporary "guest workers" or as the legacy of colonial rule. The white European was always assumed to be in a leading role in driving the societal changes towards prosperity and growth that all immigrants would gladly embrace and make their own. Somehow, since the last couple of decades, something in this social model has changed. This change has originated during the economic crisis of the early '70s. The European multicultural model grants immigrants the access to equal rights and citizenship without the necessity to learn the host nation's language, nor study the host nation's history. Naturally, because it originates in a democratic environment, the system does not demand that the immigrant give up his or her linguistic and cultural practices; it does not demand to cease intermarriage restrictions neither pressures to integrate or inter-mix with the host nation's population. Millions of migrants have been allowed to become European—using both legal and illegal procedures—on the shaky ground of asylum rights and humanitarian aid. A charitable endeavor, Christian and ecumenical in its basic belief, motivated by compassion, might have caused a frightening economic burden and a mighty source of social chaos and distress that could topple the same institutions that have promoted it. In times of crises, extraordinary measures have to be put in place in order to ensure the well-being of all involved.

It might be a painful but necessary remedy that a large number of these "new citizens" should be politely but firmly shown the door and repatriated, especially those who by holding double nationality have decided not to relinquish their original citizenship. However harsh a statement like this might sound, those who have witnessed the horrors of social strife and murderous conflict know that there are more horrors to come if some drastic measures are not taken.

What landscape for the next generation?

Immigrants are people who leave one
country, one society, and move to another
society. But there has to be a recipient
society to which the immigrants move.
— Samuel P. Huntington

For many years the Muslim communities have been social enclaves in the European landscape, too often ignored or simply dealt with as all other immigrations—with little concern. The average Muslim immigrant since the '60s and '70s was generally quiet, hard working and grateful to be accepted in the European wealthy economies. This accepted *pro takfir* attitude was likely to be a consequence of the previous turbulent years in which the African and Mediterranean countries had freed themselves from the French, Italian, German and Portuguese colonial yoke. A number of citizens of these newly independent countries, who were in disagreement with the new governments, saw the opportunity to migrate to Europe as a way to escape poverty and more civil unrest. Europe received them gladly, as the booming economy of those years was in need of additional workforce. This first generation of Muslim immigrants sought to become part of

Europe and looked keenly to integrate in Western society. The mid-'80s saw the emergence of "second-generation" Muslim communities, no longer composed of compliant and hard working migrant workers, but rather disillusioned and restless European born individuals—often disenfranchised and confined in sub-proletarian, degraded neighborhoods. Most of these young men and women were poorly educated by a system that did not know how to cater to their diversity. These new citizens began to see themselves as a permanent feature in a new Western society and developed an awareness of their rights, claiming full access to social care and equal civil opportunities and demanding equal opportunities without offering equal obedience. The first public debates on "Islam in Europe" in the late 80s surprised the public opinion. They were: "The Scarf or Veil Affair"[27] in France and the "Rushdie Fatwa" in Britain. In spite of a long historical presence of Islam in Europe, Europeans only then became aware of the Muslim communities and their uneasiness. The issue of Muslim integration started having an increasing importance on the European agendas. In the mid '80s as "Europe became the favorite grounds to escalate the Palestinian claims and terrorist attacks were perpetrated at various airports and main cities, the phenomenon of Muslim immigration became associated to terrorism."[28] Eventually, as the migration flow to the continent from Maghreb increased threefold from 1990 to 2010 and terrorist attacks were launched on European soil,

---

[27] The controversy over the Islamic scarf (hijab) sparked in October 1989, when three female students were suspended for refusing to remove their scarves in class at Gabriel Havez Middle School in Creil. In November 1989, the Conseil d'État ruled that the scarf quasi religious expression was compatible with the laïcité of public schools. That December, minister of education Lionel Jospin issued a statement declaring that educators had the responsibility of accepting or refusing the wearing of the scarf in classes on a case-by-case basis.

[28] Robert S. Leiken, "Europe's Mujahideen: Where Mass Immigration Meets Global Terrorism," Backgrounder, April 2005, Center for Immigration Studies: p. 1.

the integration of Muslim communities became extremely topical and urgent in the context of EU immigration and counter-terrorism policy. Since the terrorist attacks in Spain and in London, the full assimilation of Muslim communities as a way to fight radical Islam has become central to any government's political agenda in Europe, impacting both domestic and foreign policy.[29] The current growing role of the Muslim communities is particularly evident when European policymakers seek the opinion from European Muslim representatives—both secular and religious—before engaging in any sensitive legislation—both domestic and international.

It was when, in 2004, government ministers, responsible for integration, agreed on eleven "Common Basic Principles" that the European Union began working on immigrant consultative bodies that promoted active participation of immigrants' representatives in policy shaping. In 2005, the European Commission issued "A Common Agenda for Integration Framework for the Integration of Third-Country Nationals in the European Union."[30] Of these in particular, Common Basic Principle 7 stated that "Frequent interaction between immigrants and Member State citizens is a fundamental mechanism for integration. Shared forums, inter-cultural dialogue, education about immigrants and immigrant cultures, and stimulating living conditions in urban environments enhance the interactions between immigrants and Member State citizens."[31] Furthermore, Common Basic Principle 9 underlined that "The

---

[29]   For instance, in the issue of Turkey's EU membership, the Turkish community in Germany remained salient and has not used its collective influence to speed up the process of Turkey's membership. See Cameron, Fraser, "The Islamic Factor in the European Union's Foreign Policy," in Hunter, Shireen (ed.), Islam, Europe's Second Religion: The New Social, Cultural and Political Landscape (Center for Strategic and International Studies, Washington DC, 2002), p.262

[30]   http://ec.europa.eu/ewsi/UDRW/images/items/docl_988_232042490.pdf

[31]   Ibid.

participation of immigrants in the democratic process and in the formulation of integration policies and measures, especially at the local level, supports their integration."[32] To implement Common Basic Principle 9, the Council required all Member States to give urgent attention to political participation so that minorities would feel represented and heard. The attention from Member States had to concentrate especially to indicators of unequal levels of engagement and membership to society that are the first causes of disenfranchisement and restlessness. Structured dialogue between immigrant groups and host governments must be encouraged as a tool to stimulate participation as well as mutual understanding. In 2005, the European Commission's "Agenda on Integration" proposed the creation of "advisory platforms of third-country nationals as one way to implement this principle with national and EU policies and funding."[33] "The European Integration Fund can be used to finance dialogue platforms and consultative bodies. The second edition of the EU *Handbook on Integration* highlighted conclusions and best practices for these bodies. The European Website on Integration has also started collecting practices (ex. Strasbourg, Berlin, Piacenza)."[34] The April 2009 European Integration Forum is now considered the primary venue to give voice to the immigrant communities, to promote greater opportunities for immigrant consultation at national and EU level and "to provide a voice for representatives of civil society on integration issues, in particular relating to the EU agenda on integration, and for the Commission to take a pro-active role in such discussions."[35] When the Forum was first

---

[32]   Ibid.
[33]   Ibid.
[34]   Jacobs, D. et al., (2009). "Political participation for migrants: the MIPEX results," in Niessen, J. and Huddleston, T. (eds), Legal frameworks for the integration of third-country nationals, Nijmegen: Brill
[35]   http://ec.europa.eu/ewsi/UDRW/images/items/static_38_971048342.pdf

ideated, its participants suggested that it should concentrate on capacity building, political participation, access to EU funding for immigrant organizations and the elaboration of guidelines for the creation of consultative bodies at the national level.

Until very recently, however, the European approach did not focus specifically on countering Islamic terrorism and enforcing counter-threat security as much as it tackled the more fundamental issue of social integration of Muslim communities within European secular societies. The two approaches, although correlated, do not mirror each other in terms of short-term initiatives. Promoting acceptance and respect for the Western system of values is a long-term deterrent to religiously motivated armed struggle. Recent reaction to the terrorist onslaught has associated Western perceptions of Islam to inherent threat and fear. Many Europeans now perceive Islam as a menace to European culture and civilization as well as to the West as a whole. Even more so, after the London bombings in July 2005, the riots in the French suburbs in November 2005, the cartoon controversy in Denmark and the religiously motivated murder of a Dutch film-maker, Islam has emerged as the priority problem to be addressed. The Muslims in Europe are perceived as the alien minority that possesses cultural values and a belief system that is the most diametrically opposed to the Western tradition. These prejudices about Islam by ordinary European citizens did not occur as it often happens by mere chance. The European historical memory retains other major bloody events, such as Poitiers, the battle of Lepanto in 1574 or the Ottoman siege of Vienna in 1680. The building of the European socio economic fabric, in its Judeo-Christian identity, excluded a greater Islamic influence. Furthermore, the threat of Islamic expansion is still well present in the collective memories of a number of European countries that only achieved their independence in the nineteenth century—Greece, Bulgaria, Romania and Cyprus. The Balkan wars with its atrocities that were committed from all sides but that saw the influx of a number of multinational Jihadists was also a recent reminder of the religious conflict next door. Finally the terrorists' actions in the name of Islam contribute in creating an atmosphere of distrust and suspicion toward Muslims, causing a so-called *Islamophobia* well depicted in Huntington's theory on the "clash of civilizations."

In 1993, Samuel Huntington, a professor of political sciences at the University of Harvard, wrote an article in the journal *Foreign Affairs*, titled "The Clash of Civilizations." Huntington's article proposed a logical framework to understand most conflicts that had taken place since the end of the twentieth century attempting a forecast for the possibility of the future conflicts. Huntington claimed that the world has been in a non-ideological era since the end of the Cold War and that the role of the nation-state has been less and less significant. Consequently, civilizations are to clash with one another. Culture, and especially its religious element, has become the main cause of conflicts, far more than political objectives such as territorial conquests. Huntington asserts that "in the second half of the twentieth century, a new type of opposition has succeeded the Middle Ages conflicts between princes and the post-Westphalia antagonisms between nations". This new type of conflict is now present in a number of major civiliza-tions—the Western, the Confucian, the Japanese, the Islamic, the Hindu, the Slavic-Orthodox, the Latin American and pos-sibly now the African civilization. Huntington clearly stated that "…. the fundamental source of conflict in this new world will not be primarily ideological or primarily economic. The great divisions among human kind and the dominating source of conflict will be cultural. Nation-states will remain the most powerful actors in world affairs, but the principal conflicts of global politics will occur between nations and groups of different civilizations. The clash of civilizations will dominate global politics. The fault lines between civilizations will be the battle lines of the future. The West won the world not by the superiority of its ideas or values or religion, but rather by its superiority in applying organized violence. Westerners often forget this fact, non-Westerners never do."[36]

With the end of political ideologies, human beings would first and foremost feel a close recognizance as regards to shared cultural features such as religion and ethnicity. As a consequence, individuals "would acknowledge their belonging to one culture, or civilization. That supposition is relatively reliable because, effectively, the federation of individuals into ethno-national groups, due to tribalism in the wake of the disintegration of political unity, deeply influences world politics."[37] Very interestingly, Huntington states that the differences distinguishing civilizations do not necessarily imply the emergence of conflicts between them and, at the same time, he develops a completely opposite argument—he declares that "civilizations are intrinsically in conflict because they are driven by incompatible moral and political values, the necessity to survive, and the will to dominate. That characteristic of the new world order would be all the more disturbing because the civilizations would behave according to the kin-country syndrome, namely those civilizations would ally with more or less kin-civilizations."[38] Subsequently, conflicts would primarily break out along the fault lines between civilizations. Huntington's explanation of conflicts all over the world may seem coherent since, in

---

[36] Huntington, Samuel P., The Clash of Civilizations and the Remaking of World Order, Simon and Schuster, New York, 1996 p. 51
[37] Ibid., p. 52
[38] Ibid., p. 48

effect, numerous conflicts have arisen along his fault lines.[39] He finally describes the emergence of a conspicuous Islamic menace for the Western countries in addition to concomitant threats. Indeed, according to Huntington: "Islam has bloody borders." His perception of the borders of Islam clearly reflects the geography of religious strife and Jihad-motivated conflict. Again the bloody fighting amongst Christian and Muslim populations in the Balkans is at the forefront of his analysis. In his most hard-to-subscribe-to theory, Huntington argues that the "Islamic civilization could seek military cooperation, for instance with China, mostly due to anti-western reaction, and thus create a Confucian-Islamic Connection. Subsequently, western countries should protect themselves thanks to the establishment of fortifications in the 'torn-countries,' as in Turkey, which is located on a fault line separating two civilizations. Besides, the western countries should also ally with friendly civilizations such as the Latin-American civilization, and endeavor to destabilize hostile civilizations according to the balance-of-power."[40] The theory is tough to embrace as the likelihood that Islam could ever produce a successful intercultural connection is very limited indeed.

Aside from Huntington's clear stance on the issue, the opinions on Islam in Europe are very much split between those who support immigration and an integrated and multicultural European society and those who vehemently oppose it. The polarization of the debate raises doubts about the chance of a successful large-scale integration in the short term.

The political mainstream argues whether Islam is compatible with liberalism and democracy and whether it can be

---

[39]   Ibid., p. 45
[40]   Ibid., p. 53

reconciled with European values or not.[41] It is now becoming more and more accepted to expose the shortcomings of Islam particularly amongst the right wing and the conservative milieus. This critical stand is paying off politically during election times.[42] All of this makes it hard for moderates on both sides, native Europeans and Muslims, to remain rational and calm.

Paradoxically the most critical challenge seems not only to be Islamic assimilation but the relative fragility of Western society. Europe's social fabric has been weakened from within by decades of decline caused by economic and moral corruption and a deeply ingrained unusual cynicism that has done away with the most ethical and moral values—both religious and civic. This decline concerns politics in most of the Western world. Polarization, poor values and a complete disconnection between the political class and its base seems to be a constant in the parliaments of most Western democracies. Notwithstanding controversial economic policies and domestic issues, the decline of wise international politics has emerged with stark clarity in the occurrences surrounding the Balkans crisis and, more recently, the wars in Iraq and Afghanistan.

In both, most Europeans feel that they have been obliged not only to participate in wars that should never have been fought but also to foot the enormous bill associated with them. Europe was already reeling from the costs generated in the Balkans conflict. The recent Libyan experience has

---

[41] A striking case was the speech of Pope Benedict XVI in September 2006, where the holy Father described Islam as an aggressive religion, including in his speech the quotation calling Islam an "evil and inhuman" religion.

[42] See the proposition of the Belgian rightist party Vlaamse Belang to repatriate those immigrants who do not make the greater efforts to integrate, or the protest demonstration in Brussels on September 11, 2007, "Stop the Islamization of Europe," organized by the German right-wing organization "Pax Europa," or a release of the anti-Islamic film "Fitna" by Dutch politician and the leader of ultra-right "Party of Freedom," Geert Wilders.

confirmed that Europe no longer carries any decisive weight on the international military stage. Too often the European military policy is a pawn dictated by the strategic supremacy of the United States, China or Russia. American hegemony, heavily challenged by the economic crisis and by years of war, can do little to guarantee European security in the face of economic decline or terrorist attacks. As a result, European nations are currently finding that they serve merely to make up the numbers in the international equilibrium. Whereas new actors like China, India and Brazil are helping to define the world political stage and old actors like Russia are trying to make a comeback, Europe is slowly fading away in its ability to matter in the world. As journalist Neil Ferguson wrote when considering the fate of Western civilization: "When Kenneth Clark defined civilization in his acclaimed 1969 television series of that name, he left viewers in no doubt that he meant the civilization of the West—and primarily the art and architecture of Western Europe from the Middle Ages until the nineteenth century. Clark's hugely successful series defined civilization for a generation in the English-speaking world. Civilization was the chateaux of the Loire, the Palazzi of Florence, the Sistine Chapel, and Versailles. But then something changed. After around 1960, the word civilization slumped in popularity. Universities—beginning with Stanford in 1963—ceased to offer the classic Western Civ history course. To the generation that came of age protesting against the Vietnam War, Mahatma Gandhi had been right when he implied that "Western civilization" was a contradiction in terms. It was nothing more than a euphemism for a blood-steeped, bomb-dropping imperialism."[43] He then went on to say that "...thanks to an educationalists' fad that

---

[43]   Niall Ferguson: Why the West is now in decline, *The Telegraph*, March 6, 2011

elevated historical skills above knowledge in the name of New History—combined with the unintended consequences of the curriculum-reform process—most British teenagers now leave secondary school knowing only unconnected fragments of Western history."[44] Moreover, he keeps stating that first-year history university students interviewed at one leading British university revealed that "only 34 per cent knew who the English monarch was at the time of the Armada, 31 per cent knew the location of the Boer War and 16 per cent knew who commanded the British forces at Waterloo. In a similar poll of English children aged between 11 and 18, 17 per cent thought Oliver Cromwell fought at the Battle of Hastings."[45] Ferguson believes that the rise of the West is the pre-eminent historical phenomenon of the last millennium and, with its narrative, it is at the very heart of modern history and is what has allowed the West to separate above and beyond the rest of the world. According to Ferguson, this feat was accomplished thanks to "six identifiably specific behaviors, namely Competition, Science, Property Rights, Medicine, Consumer Society and the Work Ethic."[46] Thanks to these pillars of social development a part of mankind originating in Europe managed to dominate the world for over 500 years. This is of extreme importance for it is only by identifying the causes of European success that eventually we will predict the imminence of the European collapse. The same can be extended to the Western world—only by fully understanding the reasons for the West's incredible run we will be able to discern the causes and timing of its failure. The next generation—our children—will witness the twilight and the end of Western primacy, primarily because the Europeans

---

[44] Ibid.
[45] Ibid.
[46] Ibid.

themselves have lost faith in their own civilization. In 2009 the UK's *Financial Times* journalist Christopher Caldwell authored a pivotal book on the revolution in Europe wrought by Muslim immigration. Caldwell's book, *Reflections on the Revolution in Europe: Immigration, Islam and the West,* asserts that "European opinion leaders and elites were so affected by Holocaust guilt and anti-racism that they recklessly celebrated diversity and bred monsters in their midst. These worthy sentiments were transformed by the pressure of mass immigration so that the post-Holocaust repentance became a template for regulating the affairs of any minority that could plausibly present itself as seriously aggrieved while Europeans engaged in fear masqueraded as tolerance."[47] The main beneficiaries of Europe's ideological sickness—Caldwell argues—are Muslims, who were "a living, thriving, and confident European ethnic group with a lot of claims to press."[48] Caldwell goes beyond and blames Europe's promotion of multiculturalism as "a consequence of a self-loathing and loss of confidence that extends to religious, cultural and even sexual matters. Not only do Europeans no longer believe in anything, but immigration has made them feel 'contemptible and small, ugly and asexual"[49]. Extensive reference to Caldwell research can be found on an authoritative British website—irr.org.uk—which states that Caldwell holds that immigrants share a puritanical aversion to Europe's depraved sexual mores that might make them reluctant to integrate. Europe's third-world immigrants and particularly Muslims might not undergo the "same demographic transition that their Western hosts did—that is to have smaller families—because

---

[47]   Reflections on the Revolution in Europe: Immigration, Islam, and the West. London, Allen Lane. 2009.
[48]   Ibid.
[49]   Ibid.

Muslim culture is unusually full of messages laying out the practical advantages of procreation"[50] as preached in the most-read book in the world, the Qu'ran. Maybe the first step to understand the future of Europe should be to understand the Qu'ran itself and the people of that book.

The Qu'ran fascinates me as, like most religious texts, it is clearly the creation of one or more enlightened beings. Like the Bible or the Torah, it carries a divine message, a sublime story of love, reconciliation and redemption. What fascinates me is how humans can read in such a loving and divine narrative an order to destroy. History shows us that Christianity predates Islam in its willingness to use God's word to justify strife and Judaism predates Christianity in its willingness to use God's word to exclude others. At the end of the day, it is not the Word, it is the nature of man.

It is important to determine how the Qu'ran shapes the modern stratification of Islam and, without going into a fully fledged theological analysis, understand its historical reasons and the development of Islamic society into today's reality.

---

[50] Ibid.

The new global
identity of Islam

The ruling to kill the Americans and their allies—
civilians and military—is an individual duty for
every Muslim who can do it in any country in
which it is possible to do it, in order to liberate
al-Aqsa Mosque and the holy mosques from their
grip, and in order for their armies to move out
of all the lands of Islam, defeated and unable to
threaten any Muslim. This is in accordance with the
words of Almighty God: "And fight the pagans all
together as they fight you all together," and "Fight
them until there is no more tumult or oppression,
and there prevails justice and faith in God."

— OSAMA BIN LADEN[51]

THE WORLD GEOPOLITICAL SCENARIO dramatically changed the day of the attack on the Twin Towers in downtown New York and the subsequent GWOT—the Global War on Terrorism—waged by the United States and its NATO allies, many of which are European. Europe suddenly was forced to take sides and make a stand. With very few exceptions, on September 11th, 2001, every Caucasian European became

---

[51] Fatwa issued by Osama bin Laden and others in al-Qaeda, published in al-Quds al-Arabi, February 23, 1998.

American. Suddenly by taking sides Europe confirmed it had become the front line and one of the main battlegrounds of international terrorism, Madrid and London *docent*.[52] The occurrence of the terrorist attacks in Madrid in 2004 and in London in 2005 introduced two new security threats to the European public debate: homegrown terrorism and radicalization. In 2009, officials and analysts from the Dutch Institute of international relations went as far as stating that the "threat of terrorism did not come from far-away countries but originated in people living as fairly well integrated citizens on European soil shocked the public and sparked a wave of research into the processes of radicalization that had led the perpetrators to their actions. Since then, homegrown radicalization of young Muslims in Europe has come to constitute one of the most pressing and elusive challenges for politicians, policy makers, and scientists, who have been confronted with questions about the reasons for and the scope of radicalization."[53] Finally, full attention was given to the causes that led young disaffected Muslims to embrace violence as a tool for change instead of pursuing avenues of public representation within their national entities. Radicalization is a far too important social threat to only be tackled for fear of future kinetic attacks. The radicalization phenomenon in small social groups rarely leads to murderous exploits; however it undermines the unity of the social fabric and leads to deep-seated inequalities amongst human beings.

As the Dutch General Intelligence and Security Service (AIVD) notes in one of its reports on radicalization and

---

[52] Juan Jose Escobar Stemmann, "Middle East Salafism's Influence and the Radicalization of Muslim Communities in Europe," MERIA Journal Vol. 10 No. 3 (September 2006), p. 1.

[53] Islamist Radicalisation: A Root Cause Model, Tinka Veldhuis & Jørgen Staun, Netherlands Institute of International Relations, Clingendael, October 2009.

Salafism: "There is no threat of violence here, nor of an imminent assault upon the Dutch or Western democratic order, but this is a slow process which could gradually harm social cohesion and solidarity and undermine certain fundamental human rights."[54] The AIVD goes on to analyze that radicalization induces polarization in the social texture leading to what the AIVD defines as intolerant isolationism. The stance is that "...violent as well as non-violent radicalization can both threaten the integration and peaceful coexistence of different cultural groups within society."[55] The investigative results, all over the continent, clearly found that most of the domestic kinetic attacks were financed, planned and executed by home-grown Jihadists with limited outside coordination and support.[56] Outside support was defined as being limited only to indoctrination and training. The "Sleeping Beauty" suddenly had to wake up to a new reality: European Jihad might have non-EU provenance but it is very much a domestic problem just like the Red Brigades, the Rote Armee Fraktion, the Baader-Meinhof, Euskadi-Ta-Askatasuna and the Nuclei Armati Rivoluzionari. There was going to be no USA flagged prince savior this time; a victory in Afghanistan or Iraq was not going to solve the issue. There was going to be no Omaha Beach this time nor could there be as the new GWOT has no real front lines nor an enemy Reichstag to occupy. Since the Spanish and British capitals' attacks, even if the number of radicalized Muslims might be growing, the EU has reacted by infiltrating and deterring the next major terrorist attack. According to Europol reports—"...in 2007 the EU Member

---

[54]   Ibid.

[55]   Ibid.

[56]   For political correctness, the EU officially rejects the automatic identification of terrorism with Islam. According to a classified lexicon handbook, which offers "non-offensive" phrases, banned terms are said to include "Jihad", "Islamic" and "fundamentalist."

States arrested 201 suspects for Islamist terrorist offences; in 2009, six Member States reported 294 failed, foiled or successfully executed attacks. Furthermore, an additional 124 attacks were carried out in Northern Ireland. The number of Islamic attacks decreased by 33% in comparison to 2008 and is almost half the number of attacks carried out in 2007. In 2009, only one Islamist terrorist attack was successful directed at a military target in Italy. The majority of those arrested had the citizenship of the country of arrest."[57] To spread their ideology the Islamic movements use targeted propaganda as an important tool for attracting resources and recruits to terrorist groups, such as the Al Qaida propaganda on the Internet. Studies of the European Parliament affirm that "… these propaganda activities affect both European readers, but also terrorist cells and groups outside Europe."[58] Thus threats to European domestic security become an international threat. Many EU nationals were recruited for Jihad in Iraq and Afghanistan. "In 2007 Iraq attracted the largest number of recruits from EU Member States. The European based Islamic terrorist groups provide logistical support to terrorism world wide, providing 'Threat Financing' and false identity documents."[59]

Muslim radicalism in Europe has been primarily imported through the Islamist movements, most of which had been banned in the Middle East countries in the 1980s to be revived just before and after the Arab Spring. The following are

[57]   TE-SAT 2010-EU Terrorism Situation and Trend Report, European Police Office (Europol), Hague, 2010: p. 18–19.
[58]   Islam in the European Union: What's at Stake in the Future? Felice Dassetto, European Parliament, Policy Department Structural and Cohesion Policies, Brussels, May 2007, p. 15.
[59]   Combating the financing of terrorism: A history and assessment of the control of "threat finance," Prof. Michael Levi, University of Cardiff, British Journal of Criminology Special Issue, July 2010.

particularly active in Europe amongst the Islamist groups included in the EU Council's list of terrorist organizations: Hizballah, Jamaat al-Tabligh, Hizb ut-Tahrir and the Muslim Brotherhood. Hizballah appeared in the European Union in the '80s along with refugees from the civil war in Lebanon. "On March 10, 2005 the European Parliament passed a non-binding resolution recognizing clear evidence of terrorist activities by Hizballah. The EU Council should take all necessary steps to curtail them. The EU Council, however, has refused to act yet."[60] Hizballah is a well-organized and structured institution; it functions as a quasi-government and operates well within expatriate Lebanese-Muslim communities. The exported members of the organization are a few thousand of which around a thousand live in Germany alone. In Europe, Hizballah is engaged in terrorism and subversion financing and logistical support operations, as well as local political activities. Although the organization has not been very active in Europe for several years, it is still active in the region, primarily using Europe as a fundraising and recruiting ground. Again the disenchanted and the marginalized Muslim youth represent fertile recruiting ground from such a strong brand as Hizballah. Amongst the logistical support activities originated in Europe, the smuggling of EU passports has become a very lucrative activity. Today, in the terrorism circuit there are tens of thousands of Belgian passports carried by Jihadists. Operatives with European passports have been sent in Israel to conduct surveillance and participate in attacks.

"For the radicalization of Muslim communities and recruitment of new potential Islamic terrorists throughout

---

[60] Statement before the United States House of Representatives, Committee on Foreign Affairs Subcommittee on Europe Adding Hizballah to the EU Terrorist List, by A. Ritzmann, Senior Fellow at the European Foundation for Democracy, June 20, 2007

Europe Hizballah actively uses all the information and communication means: radio, TV and increasingly coded messages by Internet."[61] Jamaat al-Tabligh is often depicted as an Islamic reform movement with a missionary focus that counts millions of members worldwide. It does not appear on the UN nor the US list of designated terrorist groups. Like most large-sized religious movements, it has factions that are peaceful and apolitical in character and zealot components that use the organization's vast reach as a spiritual and ideological platform for Jihadism. When analyzing EU member nations, approaches to domestic radicalization, it is always useful to investigate how their enforcement agencies define the phenomenon they are tackling. For example, the Danish Intelligence Service's (PET) definition of violent radicalization is: "a process, by which a person to an increasing extent accepts the use of undemocratic or violent means, including terrorism, in an attempt to reach a specific political/ideological objective."[62] The Dutch Intelligence Service's (AIVD) broader definition of radicalization is: "the (active) pursuit of and/or support to far reaching changes in society which may constitute a danger to (the continued existence of) the democratic legal order (aim), which may involve the use of undemocratic methods (means) that may harm the functioning of the democratic legal order (effect). Supplemented by: a person's (growing) willingness to pursue and/or support such changes himself (in an undemocratic way or otherwise), or his encouraging others to do so."[63] The difference between

---

[61]   The Integration of Islam in Europe: Preventing the radicalization of Muslim diasporas and counterterrorism policy, Katrine Anspaha, Department of Political Science, University of Latvia, presented at Fourth Pan-European Conference on EU Politics, University of Latvia, Riga, Latvia, p. 25–27, September 2008
[62]   Islamist Radicalisation: A Root Cause Model, Tinka Veldhuis & Jørgen Staun, Netherlands Institute of International Relations Clingendael, October 2009
[63]   Ibid.

the two definitions is that the version offered by the Danish Intelligence Service focuses more on the action taken to attain a political or other goal—that is, the willingness to use violence. The definition by the Dutch Intelligence Service, on the other hand, is broader in the "...sense that it addresses the willingness to actively support far-reaching changes in society—by any means, also but not exclusively by violent ones."[64] Policy making and subsequent enforcement strategy is always an emanation of the country's political color but it often defines the mandate and enforcement tools that are available to counteract radicalization in the short term. A common mandate has helped the countless US enforcement and intelligence agencies to achieve a certain degree of cooperation. Europe is moving in that direction too but had been lagging a few years behind—a delay that is hardly justified because EU Member States have had to front trans-national domestic terrorism from the '60s to the '80s. The definition by the European Commission depicts violent radicalization as follows: "The phenomenon of people embracing opinions, views and ideas which could lead to acts of terrorism."[65] The common denominator amongst all the available definitions of radicalization is that it implies a gradual process that, although it can occur very rapidly, has no specifically defined beginning or end. "It is an individual development that is initiated by a combination of factors and comprises a drastic change in attitudes and behavior."[66] Although the threshold between radicalization and terrorism is very thin, it is still important to stress that these two dynamics are, in their

---

[64]   Ibid.

[65]   Communication From The Commission To The European Parliament And The Council Com (2005) 313, concerning terrorist recruitment: addressing the factors contributing to violent radicalisation, p. 2

[66]   Islamist Radicalization: A Root Cause Model, Tinka Veldhuis & Jørgen Staun, The Hague, Netherlands Institute of International Relations Clingendael, October 2009.

effects, distinct from each other. The Council of the European Union refers to terrorism as "…intentional acts that were committed with the aim of seriously intimidating a population, or unduly compelling a government or international organization to perform or abstain from performing any act, or seriously destabilizing or destroying the fundamental political, constitutional, economic or social structures of a country or an international organization."[67] Terrorist actions are defined as a "…political tool that, irrespective of their success rate, are used in an attempt to bring about political or societal change."[68] Radicalization is then a process of transformation that does not serve a clearly stated purpose and does not necessarily have to be related to violence; radicalization has no objective nor plan. Radicalization is a process, terrorism is a tool. Are violent radicalization and terrorism the same concept? Violent radicalization might include the process of adopting a belief system that promotes violent action but it does not imply that people who radicalize also *act* violently. Max Abrahms on analyzing the failure of terrorism quotes Robert Pape as one of the most influential scholars of suicide terrorism. Abrahms attributes to Pape the statement that: "terrorists are simply the members of their societies who are the most optimistic about the usefulness of violence for achieving goals that many, and often most, support."[69] In his analysis Abrahms goes on to say that in several cases, people who radicalize refrain from engaging in terrorist activity and he supports his statement by quoting Pape, "Terrorism is one of the worst possible, but nevertheless

---

[67] European Union, Council Framework Decision of June 13, 2002 on combating terrorism.
[68] Ibid.
[69] Why Terrorism Does Not Work, by Max Abrahms, International Security, Vol. 31, No. 2 (Fall 2006), pp. 42–78.

avoidable, outcomes of violent radicalization. In other words, although every terrorist is a radical, not every radical is a terrorist. This implies that radicalization processes can evolve in many directions, including non-violent ones, such as political movements and political parties—that can nevertheless be perceived as radical. For example, radicalization can prompt Muslims to become socially committed to intense dawa or missionary practices or strong religious devotion."[70] In support of Pape and Abrahms, theories is the acceptance that many Western-bred radical Muslims have been born and raised in the relative prosperity of democratic nations and some of them come from well-off, well-integrated families. That is when the difficulty in detecting potential terrorists arises as they are quite well integrated and indistinguishable from the general population. "They speak European languages, have been educated in Europe and have often had a relatively normal upbringing without—as far as one could tell—outstanding childhood traumas or conspicuous religious practices."[71] Edwin Bakker states that "research into the demographic characteristics of Jihadist terrorists in Europe and around the world has shown that these radicals were generally middle-class, educated young men who often had wives and children."[72] Violent acts perpetrated in order to satisfy the basic physiological needs of an individual are easier to counteract because needs such as the desire for food, for shelter, for opportunities and for security are easier to cater for. When violent acts are undertaken in order to satisfy a moral and intellectual perception, the challenge increases

---

[70] Ibid.

[71] Islamist Radicalization: A Root Cause Model, Tinka Veldhuis & Jørgen Staun, The Hague, Netherlands Institute of International Relations Clingendael, October 2009

[72] Edwin Bakker, Jihadi terrorism and the radicalization challenge in Europe, Rik Coolsaet, Ashgate publishing, 2008, chapter 6.

dramatically in its complexity. Radicalization among Muslims in the West often wants to be justified by the perceived suffering of their "Muslim brothers" in the Islamic world[73] and vice versa. Global Islamic radicalization seems to be an objection against perceived wrongdoing against fellow believers, rather than self-focused. Global religious partnership in suffering might be common about other religions like Judaism, but Farad Khosrokhavar—the Al Qaida theorist—claims it has been appropriated by radical Islam as "humiliation by proxy."[74] The authoritative website diis.dk covers these issues with a plethora of great details. It has been so far a great resource for monitoring of radicalization trends. It reports that "radicalized Muslims like Mohammad Siddique Khan (the alleged ringleader of the 2005 attacks on the London Tube system) and Mohammed Bouyeri (Van Gogh's murderer) have distributed video messages and other documents that invariably refer to Middle Eastern and Asian countries like Palestine and Afghanistan, where Muslims are perceived to live in a constant threat of war and humiliation. Therefore, home-grown radicalization often seems to comprise an altruistic component in the sense that, apparently, radicalizing Muslims in Europe does not necessarily mean they have to be personally deprived or victimized in order to radicalize and turn to violence as a political tool to change the status quo." The website also quotes Khosrokhavar in reference to the importance of social belonging that brings "...individuals who are in search of a satisfactory identity to be drawn to radical groups and ideologies that provide an identity as well as clear behavioral guidelines and sense of belonging."[75] It also reports the well-accepted theory that

---

[73] Ibid.

[74] Farhad Khosrokhavar, Quand Al Qaida parle, 2006, translation Eng.

[75] Ibid.

disenfranchised, second-generation Muslims who feel that they are not completely accepted by their parents' generation nor by their European peers often turn to a strong identification with the Muslim World—the Ummah. The European security website TransnationalTerrorism.eu defines allegiance and in the Islamic case to the Ummah by stating that: "The stronger there is a need to belong, the more these individuals will be vulnerable to peer pressure and norm-conformity in order to affiliate with a social group. They will be motivated to prove faith and loyalty to the common values of the group as well. As such, the need for a satisfactory social identity essentially brings forth the urge to belong to a social group." The modern sociological debate is about how influential is religion in shaping culture and how fundamental is culture in shaping the integration process.

In reality if we move away from the polarized worldview, formerly East/West or North/South—as purported by Huntington, we may observe that most of today's European-born Muslims do not identify themselves with their immediate nucleus such as their families' roots, the culture of their family's country of origin, nor the social structure of their new motherland. They identify primarily with a conceptual paradigm such as the Ummah as it possesses all the abstract benefits and nothing of the reality that they witness daily and they tend to reject. This shift from ethnic and national categories to an increasing identification with the religious and political category of "Muslim" is often found when social democracies fail to rally individuals under common moral objectives. The new generations of Muslims follow the same trend found in borderless globalization—they have a transnational identity which transcends ethnic belonging. The sudden spreading of the Arab Spring has demonstrated that the Ummah is the virtual place where Islam becomes a global unifying force for collective action, identification and political mobilization. Being a Muslim is now becoming more of a political statement than a religious one as it is increasingly a tool for branding political campaigns or as a collection effort to unite a world of dissatisfied human beings. The Ummah that at times rejects modern innovation uses technology and globalization tools to virtually abolish the borders of Kosovo, Palestine, Iraq, Afghanistan, Syria, Indonesia and Kashmir and bring all of these areas in the same conflict for space and for justice. The British Muslims (it has been suggested about them) "...they are more integrated into the global Muslim community than into the local or national politics. The first Gulf War, the conflict in Bosnia, events in Israel and the Palestine, the Taliban struggle in Afghanistan and the war in Iraq have all fueled this feeling of Muslim solidarity."[76] Also, most Muslims express their "transnational identity not just by embracing orthodox Islam but particularly through their sense of solidarity with their brothers and sisters."[77] Modern Jihadists are not old generation traditional Muslims; they do not embody a traditional culture—rather their beliefs are de-contextualized while being highly charged with universal Islamic culture.[78]

This shift to universal Islamic culture—the Ummah—centered on radicalized religious values will likely seek a confrontation against any Western universal values and culture, regardless of its secular component, European, American or Arabian. The most active in exploiting the universality of Islam across the world is the Salafist movement. In its return

---

[76] The Radicalization of Diasporas and Terrorism, ed. B. Hoffman, W. Rosenau (Zurich: RAND Corporation, 2007), p. 11.

[77] Jocelyne Cesari, "Muslim Minorities in Europe: The Silent Revolution," Modernizing Islam: Religion in the Public Sphere in the Middle East and in Europe, ed. J. Esposito and F. Burgat (Rutgers University Press, 2003), p. 135.

[78] Olivier Roy, "A Clash of Cultures or a Debate on Europe's Values?" ISIM Review 15 (Spring, 2005), p. 6.

to absolute purism, it connects members of a virtual monastic community that embodies the aspiration to full religious purification. The Salafis with their global reach are one of the fastest-growing Islamic movements worldwide. Even more moderate Islamists willingly recognize the effectiveness of the Salafi message movement and its profound effects on Islamic practice. Salafi's purism and medieval ultra-orthodoxy not only keeps appealing to those in need of meaning but is also a constant presence in the study of many practicing Muslims and in the doctrinal charters of some of the most powerful and politically heavy Islamic organizations in the world such as the Islamic Jihad, the Gamiyya Islamiyya in Egypt, the Armed Islamic Group in Algeria and the Egyptian Muslim Brotherhood. In the recent events that led to the Arab Spring, the Salafis had a leveraging effect and have positioned themselves with prominent roles in the post-regime, so-called democratic transition governments. Most identify Salafism as the ultra conservative offspring of Wahhabism.

Already in the year 2000, the Saudi state and its religious hierarchy were the "major producers and exporters of Salafi publications, literature, instructors, missionary operations and humanitarian assistance; and the transnational organization of the movement, which incorporates a myriad of nationalities, renders it an effective and influential force in the Muslim world."[79] The term "Salafi" derives from the Arabic word "Salaf" that translates to "predecessor" or "forefather," and the first three Muslim generations are collectively referred to as *"al-Salaf as-Saleh,"* or "the Pious Predecessors," who learned about Islam directly from the messenger of God or those who knew him.[80] Because of this connection to the Prophet

---

[79] The New Global Threat: Transnational Salafis and Jihad, Quintan Wiktorowicz, Middle East Policy, Vol. VIII, No. 4, December 2001
[80] http://www.as-salaf.com/article.php?aid=50&lang=en

and the divine revelations, Salafis believe that the Prophet's Companions enjoyed a pure understanding of the religion. As depicted by Quintan Wiktorowicz, in 2001, Salafis "…were sullied and distorted by the introduction of innovations (*bida*) and the development of schisms in the Muslim community, which pulled the community of the faithful away from the straight path of Islam."[81] Most have written about it but to fully understand the birth of the Salafist movement, it is truly worth it to report, almost word by word, Wiktorowicz writing on the subject as it might perhaps be considered the most accurate and synthetic compendium of this powerful movement.

> Deviations occurred with the passage of time and as Islam spread to other cultural settings outside the Arabian Peninsula they were reinforced by the incorporation of local customs. Celebrating the Prophet's birthday, visiting the tombs of saints, and various Sufi rituals are popular practices that are openly criticized as deviations that threaten the purity of the message as revealed by the Prophet. The goal of the Salafi movement is to eradicate these innovations by returning to the pure form of Islam practiced by the Prophet and his Companions. To foster this purification, all decisions and actions in life must be based upon direct evidence from the sources of the religion: the Qu'ran and the Sunnah (path or traditions of the Prophet Mohammed). "Salafis have therefore developed a manhaj or method for determining proper religious interpretations based upon the Qu'ran, the Sunnah, and the example of the Companions."[82]

---

[81] The New Global Threat: Transnational Salafis and Jihad, Quintan Wiktorowicz, Middle East Policy, Vol. VIII, No. 4, December 2001
[82] Ibid.

This includes searching for evidence in authentic *hadiths* (the written record of the Prophet's Sunnah), as detailed by the Companions; a rejection of popular practices not explicitly outlined in the Qu'ran or Sunnah; emphasis on "worshiping only God *(tawhid)*; and a rejection of the four separate schools of Islamic jurisprudence *(mathhabs)* that divide Muslims, since there can only be one right religious answer and ruling—that which is according to God as outlined in the sources of the religion."[83] In pursuing this approach, Salafis hope to construct a transnational community of true believers whose immutable adherence to the faith will be rewarded with salvation. Those who follow this manhaj are considered Salafis. The Salafi approach has clashed with a number of other Islamic sects, which are often decried as un-Islamic. "Sufis, in particular, have incurred the wrath of Salafi purists, who argue that popular Sufi practices and rituals constitute heresy. In particular, the use of saints as intermediaries in prayer is condemned as ascribing partners to God in worship (shirk), an act vehemently prohibited in the Qu'ran."[84] Salafis argue that the Prophet did not sanction these behaviors and consequently have devoted much of their collective energy combating Sufism and other sects viewed as deviating from the straight path of Islam. Disagreements between Salafis and Sufis over such issues have led to discursive conflicts through publications, cassettes, the Internet and missionary activities. At times these confrontations have led to violent Salafi attacks against

---

[83]   Ibid.
[84]   Ibid.

Sufi mosques, leaders and followers. Salafi missionary activities, especially in Central Asia where Sufism is prevalent, have frequently met with resistance by local religious authorities, who view Salafi puritanicalism as antithetical to local understandings, often labeling it Wahhabism to connote its foreign Saudi origins. Because of a sense of certainty in the search for religious truth, as outlined by evidence in the Qu'ran and Sunnah, there is little attempt to bridge differences with other Islamic sects and groups. Nor is there any ecumenical tendency within the Salafi movement. Instead, Salafis believe that there is only one accurate religious truth as revealed by the Prophet Muhammad, and any differences of interpretation are considered deviations from Islam. Because Salafis believe they approximate the practices endorsed by the Prophet, they believe they are the only group that will be saved on Judgment Day. This is based on various *hadiths,* including: "And this Ummah (the Muslim community) will divide into 73 sects all of which except one will go to Hell, and they, the saved sect, are those who are upon what I and my Companions are upon."[85] As a result, the Salafi movement presents a forceful front of missionary appeal without adopting ideas from other sects, groups or movements. This certainty and uncompromising stance have led others in the Muslim community to label Salafis as stubborn radicals. This orientation constitutes the foundation for the religious beliefs and understandings of the late Bin Laden and other Salafis who exalt violence in the name of

---

[85]   As purported in the Islamic network site: http://www.islaam.net/main/display.php?id=72&category=73

Islam. These "Jihadi" Salafis identify themselves as adherents to the Salafi manhaj and use well-known Salafi identity markers such as *Ahl al-Hadith* (People of Hadith), *taifat al-mansura* (the Aided Group), *al-firqa al-najiyya* (the Saved Sect), and "those who follow the creed or way of the Sunnah and Jamaa."[86] As a result, the arguments supporting the use of violence conscientiously implement the Salafi manhaj and devote considerable effort to locating the religious evidence needed to legitimize particular conflicts, actions and decisions. In his 1996 Declaration of War against the United States the late Bin Laden carefully justified the use of violence through quotations of the Qu'ran and authentic *hadiths*, citing pieces of evidence according to the Salafi manhaj and praising publications by other well-known Salafis, such as Safar al-Hawali, a Saudi religious scholar known for his opposition to the US military presence in Saudi Arabia.

This lengthy extract from Quintan Wiktorowicz's work frames Salafism and its relationship with traditional Saudi Wahhabism that it aims to substitute as the orthodox current attracting the disaffected and seeking a community of identity.

The ongoing process of globalization has proven beneficial for the spreading of market economy, notwithstanding it has also facilitated the emergence of transnational Islamic movements, which can today easily reach large communities across the world, spreading messages, recruiting new followers and organizing collective activities. Wiktorowicz outlines how the "transnational Salafi movement connects Muslims

---

[86]   The New Global Threat: Transnational Salafis and Jihad, Quintan Wiktorowicz, Middle East Policy, Vol. VIII, No. 4, December 2001

into a virtual community through a common approach to Islam."[87] Wiktorowicz has been appointed in January 2011 by the White House as the senior director for global engagement at the National Security Council, positioning him as one of the most knowledgeable advisors on the subject of Islam, to President Obama. He claims Transnational indoctrination is a by-product of globalization and symbolizes the rapid expansion of transnational, virtual networks that serve as platforms for transnational opinion formation and recruitment into radical movements."[88] Is globalization a tool for democratic development and a consequence of the freedom that the world's population seeks or a source conflict between ethnically, culturally or religiously diverse groups? My experience in Afghanistan, a profoundly devout nation, taught me how the effect of globalizing tools such as the World Wide Web and a Western-styled media can become an extremely offensive instrument with its offering of readily available pornography or reality shows. The war economy that exports Western-style capitalism in a medieval, barter-based, landlocked country is another example of the trauma that can be caused by the borderless system. To this extent Islamist expert Benjamin Barber confirms that "the aggressive force of modernization and globalization dissolves social and economic barriers and exports capitalism to all parts of the world."[89] Barber calls this unstoppable mechanism: "McWorld." As a result, all of the world's communities are now confronted with a system that used to be the sole domain of Western nations: consumerism, freedom of expression, emancipation and technologies. These apparent advantages are coming at a dire price as the

---

[87]   Quintan Wiktorowicz, Radical Islam Rising: Muslim Extremism in the West, Rowman & Littlefield, 2005

[88]   Ibid.

[89]   Benjamin R. Barber, Jihad Versus McWorld, Times Books, 1995.

gap between the rich and the poor is widening in every single world's country. Therefore, globalization not only increases economic deprivation for lower-class societies and promotes wealth disparity but also confronts Muslim communities with values that were originally refuted by the Qu'ran. According to Barber, the Islamic fundamentalists believe that "Islam cannot co-exist with the Western form of modernism, and perceive the rapid rise of Westernization as an attempt by the Western world to gain control over the Islamic world."[90] Many Islamic migrants refuse the value of their new (Western) society and choose to live on its social margins if not even outside of it—this is particularly true for illegal immigrants who couple the need with will to stay off the records. As a result, Muslim communities become radicalized and nurture *mullahs* prone to instigating against the perverted Western values. Radicalization of Muslim identity is a reaction to the social exclusion, unemployment and discrimination. As reality shows, discrimination and social exclusion tend to unite migrants around religious beliefs, which influence their political participation and mobilization, and ultimately leading towards politics by another means, such as world-wide terrorism.[91] Unlike those who migrated to North America a century ago, migrants to post-war Europe found highly developed welfare states. "The entrepreneurial instincts of those who left their home countries to earn money abroad is stifled by a society that attempts to protect people against every conceivable risk."[92] Indeed Scheffer was amongst the first to denounce conflict avoidance in Europe and particularly in the Netherlands, which—he says—"has for decades closed its

---

[90]   Islamist Radicalization: A Root Cause Model, Tinka Veldhuis & Jørgen Staun, The Hague, Netherlands Institute of International Relations Clingendael, October 2009, p. 34.

[91]   Striking example is the Madrid bombings, the main result of which was European withdrawal from Iraq, first Spain and then Italy and Poland.

[92]   Immigrant Nations, Paul Scheffer, May 2011, Polity Press

eyes to the social reality of immigrant ghettos that breed high crime and unemployment."[93] A less-dense social safety net in America may be one of the reasons why immigrants generally find it easier to integrate there than in Europe, although cultural and political reasons clearly play a role as well. In Germany, even German-born children or grandchildren of immigrants often find it difficult to be accepted as full citizens if they carry a Turkish or Arab name. Scheffer is right to say that "the debate on immigration and integration 'confronts societies with their own failings.'"[94] As Scheffer points out, "anxieties about integration were as acute a century ago, when millions of Irish, Polish and Italian Catholics emigrated to North America or to the Protestant countries of northwestern Europe. A Sicilian Catholic may have been as culturally alien to local New Yorkers back then as an Anatolian Muslim is today to local Amsterdamers (or, for that matter, even to the upper classes of Istanbul and Ankara). Yet such comparisons do nothing to blunt the anti-immigration feelings that seem to have become an enduring feature of political life in Western Europe. Just because mass immigration helped the US become what it is today does not mean that Europe is likely to see a similar outcome—or even survive it."[95]

The disillusion and refusal of the hosting culture by the first- and second-generation Muslim immigrants in Europe is the premise for further political and religious engagement. The Jamaat al-Tabligh and the Muslim Brotherhood are two powerful Islamic movements that have been known to provide bodies to radicalized group. With most of their religious and political activity finding forums in mosques and madrassas, the movement's message is disseminated through interaction,

---

[93]   Ibid.
[94]   Ibid.
[95]   Ibid.

networking, common study and prayer. Western intelligence services indicate Jamaat al-Tabligh as a platform that militants use to freely travel around Europe without arousing suspicion. A report from the Guardia Civil confirmed that on January 19, 2008, the Spanish police "arrested 14 Pakistani and Indian individuals belonging to the Jamaat al-Tabligh for planning to carry out suicide bomb attacks in Barcelona and other European cities."[96] Muriel Degauque, also believed to be traveling as a Jamaat al-Tabligh's volunteer, was the first European woman to execute a suicide attack in Iraq. She was born a Belgian Catholic and died as an Islamist martyr in an explosion deep inside Iraq on November 9, 2005. She concluded her life by detonating a shrapnel-and-bearings-laden explosive vest in an attack on a US military patrol in Baquba. From the enforcement agency of her native country, the Belgium's Federal Police, the description of the transformation from a small-town Catholic girl into a Jihadi willing to take her own life in order to inflict casualties an incomprehensible deed. A transformation which can only be explained by the enormous pressure that she experienced to prove her allegiance and loyalty to her husband Issam Goris, a member of the Jamaat al-Tabligh network.[97] The husband/wife relationship and its influence on the indoctrination and radicalization of the individual have also been witnessed in Iraq where children and women have been used in suicide attacks on troops of the coalition. While most of these conversions might seem a result of embracing radicalization they are merely gestures to please religious husbands, fathers or in-laws. A small number of women and children are induced

---

[96] The Integration of Islam in Europe: Preventing the radicalization of Muslim diasporas and counterterrorism policy, Katrine Anspaha, Department of Political Science, University of Latvia, Paper prepared for the ECPR Fourth Pan-European Conference on EU Politics, University of Latvia, Riga, Latvia, pp. 25–27, September 2008

[97] http://news.bbc.co.uk/2/hi/europe/4491334.stm

(and used) to embrace the ideology of their fundamentalist husbands or fathers. The attraction seems to come from the spiritual connotation of the endeavor and by the allure of the different. For some others, conversion and radicalization is a political statement, a confirmation of will, the willingness to embrace a cause in return for attention. Craig S. Smith of the *New York Times* defines them as "…people rebelling against a society in which they feel they don't belong." Even if this is a phenomenon not only present in Islamic culture, the need for the ultimate sacrifice and to take the lives of innocents, in this case the act seems prevalently justified by the misreading of the Qu'ran. Alain Grignard, a senior official in the anti-terrorism division of the Belgian police defines them as "… people searching through a religion like Islam for a sense of solidarity. Many such women married men connected to the first wave of Europe's militant Islamists in the late 1990s, some of whom followed their husbands to Taliban-ruled Afghanistan. While they supported their husbands' militancy they never acted themselves."[98] French anti-terrorism enforcement sources predicted that female converts represent a small but very militant part of the European Jihad. In May 2003, French anti-terror investigator Judge Jean-Louis Bruguière warned that "… European terrorist networks were trying to recruit Caucasian women to handle terrorist logistics because they would be less likely to raise suspicion."[99]

The Muslim Brotherhood movement is somewhat more complex and more political. Hizb al-Ikhwan al-Muslimun has profoundly influenced the political life of Egypt and the entire Middle East since the early 1930s with its motto: "Allah is our objective. The Prophet is our leader. The Qu'ran is our

---

[98]   Police try to fathom Belgian's path to terror, by Craig S. Smith, *New York Times,* December 6, 2005
[99]   Ibid.

law. Jihad is our way. Dying in the way of Allah is our highest hope."[100] While the Brotherhood's radical ideas have shaped the beliefs of generations of Islamists over the past two decades, it had initially lost some of its power and appeal in the Middle East due to the harsh repression from local regimes and was snubbed by the younger generations of Islamists who, with the Afghanistan and Iraqi wars going on, preferred more radical organizations. In May 2011 the Brotherhood adapted its modus operandi founding the Freedom and Justice Party and participating in the Egyptian elections in November 2011. In 2010 the Brotherhood, under its original brand, had won a single seat but in the most recent elections it has won a majority of the seats. The Council on Foreign Relations is now considering the Brotherhood as the world's most influential Islamist organization. According to Lorenzo Vidino of *Middle East Quarterly*, "Muslim Brotherhood members and sympathizers have moved to Europe and slowly but steadily established a wide and well-organized network of mosques, charities and Islamic organizations. Unlike the larger Islamic community, the Muslim Brotherhood's ultimate goal may not be simply to help Muslims be the best citizens they can be, but rather to extend Islamic law throughout Europe and the United States."[101] Popular support for the Brotherhood is not monolithic; it varies across demographic factors such as age and social class, the rebirth of the movement has possibly been caused by the new "broadly centrist" posture, as defined by the Carnegie Endowment for International Peace. However, many, including Egyptian citizens, are skeptical of the centrist claims and see, in the calls by some Egyptian salafis to "tune down the harsh tones," just a pretense to gain the favors of

---

[100] The Muslim Brotherhood's Conquest of Europe, by Lorenzo Vidino, Middle East Quarterly, Winter 2005, pp. 25–34
[101] Ibid.

those who are turned off by aggressive attitudes. Vidino himself states that "…four decades of teaching and cultivation have paid off. The student refugees who migrated from the Middle East forty years ago and their descendants now lead organizations that represent the local Muslim communities in their engagement with Europe's political elite. Funded by generous contributors from the Persian Gulf, they preside over a centralized network that spans nearly every European country. These organizations represent themselves as mainstream, even as they continue to embrace the Brotherhood's radical views and maintain links to terrorists. With moderate rhetoric and well-spoken German, Dutch, and French, they have gained acceptance among European governments and media alike. Politicians across the political spectrum rush to engage them whenever an issue involving Muslims arises or, more parochially, when they seek the vote of the burgeoning Muslim community. However, when speaking Arabic or Turkish before their fellows Muslims, the 'Brothers' drop their facade and embrace radicalism."[102] Vidino goes on to say that "…while their representatives speak about interfaith dialogue and integration on television, their mosques preach hate and warn worshippers about the evils of Western society. While they publicly condemn the murder of commuters in Madrid and school children in Russia, they continue to raise money for Hamas and other terrorist organizations. Europeans, eager to create a dialogue with their increasingly disaffected Muslim minority, overlook this duplicity. The case is particularly visible in Germany, which retains a place of key importance in Europe, not only because of its location at the heart of Europe, but also because it played host to the first major wave of Muslim Brotherhood immigrants in

---

[102] Ibid.

Munich and is host to the best-organized Brotherhood presence. The German government's reaction is also instructive if only to show the dangers of accepting Muslim Brotherhood rhetoric at face value, without looking at the broader scope of its activities."[103] According to recounts of Udo Ulfkotte, rooting of the Brotherhood in Germany dates back to 1989, when—under the auspices of Abdullah at-Turki, powerful dean of Bin Saud University in Riyadh—the Saudis created the Islamische Konzil Deutschland (Islamic Council of Germany).[104] Also, according to commentator Lydia Khalil and to the *Wall Street Journal*, as recently as 2006, members of Parliament elected through the Brotherhood were openly advocating Jihad, as a reaction to Europe, and the use of violence against the United States is still advocated at public debates by members of the organization.

The following bulk of documental support can be easily found in the very authoritative forum: meforum.org, which is a must-read open source for any individual interested in the subject. The forum comes with useful references and constitutes a very interesting debating platform for many Islamism experts.

— While an official German parliament report describes the Islamische Konzil as just "another Sunni organization," such an assumption indicates a dangerous misunderstanding of the Saudi relationship to German Islamists.[105] The trend toward consolidation took a step forward in 1994 when German Islamists realized that a united coalition translated into greater political relevance and influence. Nineteen organizations, including the IGD, the Islamic Center of Munich, and the Islamic Center of Aachen, created an umbrella

---

[103] Ibid.
[104] Ulfkotte, *Der Krieg in unseren Staedten*, p. 164
[105] Ibid., p. 162

organization, the Zentralrat der Muslime. According to a senior German intelligence official, at least nine out of these nineteen organizations belong to the Muslim Brotherhood.[106] The German press investigated the Zentralrat president, Nadeem Elyas, a German-educated Saudi physician and an official of the Islamic Center of Aachen. *Die Welt* linked Elyas to Christian Ganczarski, an Al Qaida operative currently jailed as one of the masterminds of the 2002 attack on a synagogue in Tunisia.[107] Ganczarski, a German of Polish descent who converted to Islam, told authorities that Al Qaida recruited him at the Islamic University of Medina where Elyas sent him to study.[108] Elyas said he could not remember meeting him but did not deny the possibility that Ganczarski, who never completed high school, might have been one of the many individuals he had sent over the years to radical schools in Saudi Arabia.[109] Saudi donors paid all of Ganczarski's expenses.[110] Ganczarski was not alone. Elyas admitted to having sent hundreds of German Muslims to study at one of the most radical universities in Saudi Arabia.[111] The Zentralrat, which portrays itself as the umbrella organization for German Muslim organizations, has become, together with the IGD and Milli Görüş, the de facto representative of three million German Muslims. Even though the IGD is a member of the Zentralrat, the two organizations often operate independently. According to Vidino, their apparent independence

---

[106] Hartwig Mueller, Head of the Verfassungsschutz of Nordrhein Westfahlen, interview on German television SWR, Mar. 21, 2003

[107] Djerba-Anschlag: Zentralrat der Muslime gerät ins Zwielicht, Ahmet Senyurt *Die Welt* (Berlin), May 6, 2003

[108] The Muslim Brotherhood's Conquest of Europe, by Lorenzo Vidino, Middle East Quarterly, Winter 2005

[109] Ibid.

[110] Djerba-Anschlag: Zentralrat der Muslime gerät ins Zwielicht, Ahmet Senyurt *Die Welt* (Berlin), May 6, 2003

[111] Ibid.

is planned. "With many organizations operating under different names, the Muslim Brotherhood led politicians to believe they are consulting a spectrum of opinion."[112] The media seek the Zentralrat's officials when they want the Muslim view on everything from the debate about the admissibility of the *hijab* (headscarf) in public schools, to the war in Iraq, and so forth. Politicians seek the Zentralrat's endorsement when they want to reach out to the Muslim community. Many German politicians are uninformed about Islam and do not understand that the view and the interpretation of Islam that the Zentralrat expresses, as does the IGD and Milli Görüş, is that of the Muslim Brotherhood and not that of traditional Islam. Accordingly, the Zentralrat expresses total opposition to any ban of the *hijab*, supports Wahhabi-influenced Islamic education in schools, and endorses a radical position on the Middle East situation. While many Muslims endorse these views, the problem is that the Zentralrat neither represents nor tolerates those with divergent views. Moderate German Muslim groups lack the funding and organization of Muslim Brotherhood-linked groups. In terms of numbers, influence on the Muslim community, and political relevance, the Zentralrat and its two most important constituent parts, the IGD and Milli Görüş, dominate the scene. With ample Saudi financing, the Muslim Brotherhood has managed to become the voice of the Muslims in Germany. Recently, the German public was shocked to hear what is preached inside Saudi-funded mosques and schools. In the fall of 2003, a hidden camera-equipped journalist from Germany's ARD television infiltrated the Saudi-built King Fahd Academy in Bonn and taped what it taught to young Muslim children. One

---

[112] The Muslim Brotherhood's Conquest of Europe, by Lorenzo Vidino, Middle East Quarterly, Winter 2005

teacher called for Jihad against the infidels.[113] While the images elicited a rebuke from German politicians, the rather sterile debate about Saudi influence on German Muslims has not effected tangible change. Saudi officials and Saudi-run nongovernmental organizations continue to groom Muslim Brotherhood organizations. While the Muslim Brotherhood and their Saudi financiers have worked to cement Islamist influence over Germany's Muslim community, they have not limited their infiltration to Germany. Thanks to generous foreign funding, meticulous organization, and the naïveté of European elites, Muslim Brotherhood-linked organizations have gained prominent positions throughout Europe. In France, the extremist Union des Organizations Islamiques de France (Union of Islamic Organizations of France) has become the predominant organization in the government's Islamic Council.[114] In Italy, the extremist Unione delle Comunita' ed Organizzazioni Islamiche in Italia (Union of the Islamic Communities and Organizations in Italy) is the government's prime partner in dialogue regarding Italian Islamic issues.[115] In parallel to European Union integration efforts, the Muslim Brotherhood is also seeking to integrate its various European proxies. Over the past fifteen years, according to Renzo Guolo, the "Muslim Brotherhood has created a series of pan-European organizations such as the Federation of Islamic Organizations in Europe, in which representatives from national organizations can meet and plan initiatives."[116] Perhaps the Muslim Brotherhood's greatest pan-European impact has, as with the Islamische Gemeinschaft

---

[113] *Time*, Nov. 2, 2003
[114] The Muslim Brotherhood's Conquest of Europe, by Lorenzo Vidino, Middle East Quarterly, Winter 2005
[115] Renzo Guolo, *Xenofobi e Xenofili. Gli Italiani e l'Islam* (Bari: Laterza Publishing, 2003)
[116] The Global Community," MABOnline, Muslim Association of Britain, Dec. 20, 2004

Deutschland, been with its youth organization. In June 1996, Muslim youth organizations from Sweden, France, and England joined forces with the Federation of Islamic Organizations in Europe and the World Assembly of Muslim Youth to create a European Islamic youth organization.[117] Three months later, thirty-five delegates from eleven countries met in Leicester and formally launched the Forum of European Muslim Youth and Student Organizations (FEMYSO), which maintains its headquarters in Brussels.[118] According to its official website "…the Forum of European Muslim Youth and Student Organisations was established on September 1, 1996. Its mission is to be a platform for youth organizations to congregate, exchange information, gain experience and benefit from each other, to work for a better Europe. FEMYSO has developed into a wide network of 39 member organizations, bringing together youth from over 22 countries. Over the last 10 years it has become the de facto voice of Muslim Youth in Europe and is regularly consulted on issues pertaining to Muslims in Europe. FEMSO has developed useful links with the European Parliament, the Council of Europe, the United Nations and a host of other relevant organisations at the European and international level. Furthermore, it is currently a member of the Advisory Council for Youth of the Council of Europe."[119] Because the Muslim Brotherhood provides the bulk of FEMYSO's constituent organizations, in reality it strongly influences the Muslim youth in Europe."[120] While FEMYSO claims that it "is committed to fighting prejudices at all the levels, so that the future of Europe is a multicultural,

---

[117] http://www.esib.org/index.php/About%20ESU/History.html

[118] Ibid.

[119] http://www.esib.org/index.php/About%20ESU/associates/106-forum-of-european-muslim-youth-and-student-organisation-femyso.html

[120] Ibid.

inclusive and respectful one,"[121] such statements ring hollow given the position of sponsors like the World Assembly of Muslim Youth which according to Steven Emerson, believes that "the Jews are enemies of the faithful, God, and the Angels; the Jews are humanity's enemies. … Every tragedy that inflicts the Muslims is caused by the Jews."[122] The Muslim Brotherhood's ample funds and organization have contributed to their success in Europe. But their acceptance into main-stream society and their unchallenged rise to power would not have been possible had European elites been more vigilant, valued substance over rhetoric, and understood the motivations of those financing and building these Islamist organizations. Why have Europeans been so naïve? Bassam Tibi, a German professor of Syrian descent and an expert on Islam in Europe, thinks that "Europeans—and Germans in particular—fear the accusation of racism."[123] Extremists in sheep's clothing can silence almost everybody with the accusation of xenophobia. Any criticism of Muslim Brotherhood-linked organizations is followed by outcries of racism and anti-Muslim persecution. In some cases, politicians simply fail to check the backgrounds of those who claim to be legitimate representatives for the Muslim community. In other cases, politicians realize that these organizations are not the ideal counterparts in a constructive dialogue but do not take the time to seek other less visible but more moderate organizations, several of which exist only at the grassroots level, impeded by financial constraints. As Lorenzo Vidino rightly put it "…what most European politicians fail to understand

---

[121] http://www.esib.org/index.php/About%20ESU/associates/106-forum-of-european-muslim-youth-and-student-organisation-femyso.html
[122] Steven Emerson, Executive Director, statement to the National Commission on Terrorist Attacks upon the United States, July 9, 2003; See http://www.wamy.org/
[123] Bassam Tibi, *Islamische Zuwanderung, Die gescheiterte Integration* (Munich: DVA, 2002), p. 135.

is that by meeting with radical organizations, they empower them and grant the Muslim Brotherhood legitimacy."[124] There is an implied endorsement to any meeting, especially when the same politicians ignore moderate voices that do not have access to generous Saudi funding. This creates a self-perpetuating cycle of radicalization because the greater the political legitimacy of the Muslim Brotherhood, the more opportunity it and its close groups will have to influence and radicalize various European Muslim communities. The ultimate irony is that Muslim Brotherhood founder Hassan al-Banna dreamed of spreading Islamism throughout Egypt and the Muslim world, but never dreamed that his vision might also become a reality in Europe.

Another suspicious Islamist organization, Hizb ut-Tahrir, may not be fully involved in terrorism and political violence, but according to Juan José Escobar Stemmann, "it works as thought of as a conveyor belt for terrorists":[125] through indoctrination of individuals with radical ideology for the further their recruitment by the more extremist groups. Hizb ut-Tahrir is banned in most of the Muslim countries, as well as in some European countries, nonetheless it operates freely in the United Kingdom, where it radicalizes the British Muslim youth. According to Escobar, the three risk groups are targeted by the recruiters in particular: "first-generation Muslims, second or third-generation Muslims and the converts."[126] We can distinguish three different types of Muslim immigrant terrorists. The first are so called "insiders,"[127] those who

---

[124] The Muslim Brotherhood's Conquest of Europe, by Lorenzo Vidino, Middle East Quarterly, Winter 2005.

[125] Juan Jose Escobar Stemmann, "Middle East Salafism's Influence and the Radicalization of Muslim Communities in Europe," MERIA Journal, Vol. 10 No. 3 (September 2006), p. 5.

[126] Ibid., p. 9.

[127] Ibid., p. 9.

were born and educated in Europe, second-third generation Muslims, who have gained European citizenship, but in searching of identity, became alienated, re-Islamized and radicalized. For instance, in the case of July 7, 2007 bombings, the bombers were all British residents, young British Muslim men. In the case of March 11, 2004, some of the terrorists were well-integrated into the Spanish community. These suicide bombers appear to have been radicalized while living in Europe. The second are "outsiders", those who have immigrated to Europe in recent time, to study or to work, planning to become terrorists. They are foreign dissidents and asylum seekers, or radical imams who hail from Muslim countries and who preach extreme Islamism.[128] The third are converts and new Muslims.[129] As Robert Leiken explains, "there are normally second-generation citizens that speak fluently their adopted country's language and are apparently integrated through schooling and work."[130] For instance, Muhammad Atta, who led the attacks of September 11, and the killer of the Dutch filmmaker Theo van Gogh, Mohammed Bouyeri, both became radical while living in Europe and showing no apparent signs of dissidence or violence against the surrounding environment.

Detecting possible Islamists with murderous intent is not easy to do in societies where sleeper terrorist have an ability to transition in and out of normal lifestyles. This has proven a very difficult challenge for most European enforcement agencies.

---

[128] Ibid., p. 10

[129] Russell Hardin, "Politics without compromise: immigrant terrorism," prepared for delivery at the 2007 Annual Meeting of the American Political Science Association, August 30th–September 2nd, 2007: p. 8; Olivier Roy, "A Clash of Cultures or a Debate on Europe's Values?" ISIM Review 15 (Spring, 2005): p. 6

[130] Robert S. Leiken, "Europe's Mujahideen: Where Mass Immigration Meets Global Terrorism," Backgrounder, April 2005, Center for Immigration Studies, p. 7

Is multiculturalism in Europe even possible?

If once the people become inattentive to the
public affairs, you and I, and Congress and
Assemblies, Judges and Governors, shall all
become wolves. It seems to be the law of our
general nature, in spite of individual exceptions.

— THOMAS JEFFERSON

INDEPENDENTLY FROM THE success or failure of the policies to prevent illegal immigration and Islamic radicalization, the real issue at stake for Europe in the next decades is whether a multicultural society is possible at all, and if so, at what social and political cost. When thinking of the politics of multiculturalism, it is important to bear in mind that multiculturalism was the product of leftist political influence in the sixties, and reflects a conviction that all men are fungible in so much as the *homo faber*—or the worker is the only dimension that matters—cultural differences are a capitalist device to keep the working class divided. In the 1980s some mass media opinion makers tried to defend the advent of the term multiculturalism as a new, positive way to speak about diversity. In some sense this is true. But it was not by chance that the term multiculturalism was coined in the mid- to late 1980s, when race-based preferences and quotas, particularly in the USA, were coming under increasing public and legal scrutiny. At that time, the arguments for remedying past discrimination and forcing racial parity in schools and businesses were failing to persuade the American people. The website straussza.com quotes Professor Thomas L. Krannawitter of the Claremont Institute as stating that, "in their desperate search for a new defense of the discriminatory policies of affirmative action, liberals concocted the notion that without race based preferences and quotas; there would be no diversity in the classroom and workplace. Multiculturalism was intended to lend academic authority to the racial politics of affirmative action, as multicultural centers and departments began to spring up in colleges and universities around America." This became the political driver for multiculturalism, which in later years spilled over to the European continent, beginning in the UK.

While in the US since 2003 political analysts such as Krannawitter admitted that "intellectually, multiculturalism is indefensible" and "it is embarrassingly inconsistent," in Europe multiculturalism became the politically correct approach to the building of the new European Union. Coming from countries with a strong single cultural tradition, most European governments looked at the possibility offered by the multicultural approach as the perfect angle to tackle the newly forming European culture. In fact the greatest challenge for Europe in the 1990s was the affirmation of Europe as a determined political entity, belonging to no one culture but encompassing all European cultures. Building on this cultural open-door policy, Europe wanted to convey the positive elements of multiculturalism, especially when having to assimilate simultaneously 10 very politically, culturally and economically diverse and divergent countries in 2004.[131] In 2007 two more countries entered the European Union, Romania and Bulgaria, adding to the Babel of multiculturalism with an additional 2.5 million Romas—living primarily in Romania. According to the *Encyclopedia Britannica*, Roma are nomadic people "often referred to as Gypsies who live primarily in Southern and Eastern Europe. It is an ethnicity that historically had always issues in integrating with local population due to its lack or permeability and strong sense of belonging to the family that lead to family breeding." Only about one-third of children continue studies into the secondary level. This is far lower than the more than 90% proportion of non-Roma children who continue studies at an intermediate level. The situation is made worse by the fact that a large proportion of young Roma are professionally unqualified and their higher unemployment rates cause poverty, widespread social problems and crime.

As Krannawitter explained, "politically, multiculturalism is dangerous. Multiculturalism represents nothing less than the political suicide of the West."[132] Multiculturalism attempts to undermine the Judeo-Christian values upon which Europe is built, and it is corrosive of the sense of belonging that fuels participative citizenship. Multiculturalism is the end result of a process that started a long time ago, when Western philosophy turned to a state of self-destruction. Modern thinkers felt that many premises of philosophy are indemonstrable and, in particular, man cannot prove the root cause of his own freedom that is, as soon as man's freedom is understood to

---

[131] On January 1, 2004, 10 new Member States entered the EU; namely Poland, Estonia, Latvia, Lithuania, Check Republic, Slovakia, Slovenia, Hungary, Cyprus and Malta.

[132] The Intellectual Errors and Political Dangers of Multiculturalism, by Prof. Thomas L. Krannawitter, The Claremont Institute, Political Writings, February 2003

be the effect of one or more causes, it is no longer freedom. Thus modern Western philosophy began to question true man's freedom, abandoning the search for objective truth in favor of researching the causes of human thought and behavior, whether biological (e.g., Darwinism), economic (e.g., Marxism) or psychological (e.g., Freudianism). Though they disagree on the precise causes, these modern doctrines agree on the basic premise that human thought is nothing but an effect of some other mechanism, and that there is no truth to be discovered in the human mind. As Krannawitter put it, "multiculturalism is an offshoot of modern anthropology, which in itself is a product of this self-denying Western philosophy." Anthropology, and consequently multiculturalism, were extolled in the work of Jean-Jacques Rousseau, an eighteenth-century thinker and writer who openly rejected the foundation of classic thought, and whose influence continues to dominate modern European political thought. Rousseau believed that man by nature is not rational. Prior to political life, in what Rousseau called the "state of nature," men were solitary beings, having little or no interaction with one another. Therefore, argued Rousseau, pre-political, solitary man lacked language, because he had no need for language; and if man did not possess language, he could not possess reason.[133] For Rousseau, man by nature is not altogether different than an irrational being. Man began to speak, and therefore think, by some chance natural catastrophe, such as an earthquake or volcano, that brought men together and forced them to interact with one another. From Rousseau's premise, the very nature of language and the elements of human thought reflect nothing but the environmental and cultural forces that produced them. All human language and human thought—moral,

---

[133] http://www.claremont.org/publications/pubid.480/pub_detail.asp

political and religious—are the varying and purposeless effects of varying and purposeless physical causes. Inter alia, on Rousseau's theoretical hypothesis built the modern discipline of anthropology, which is the study of human cultures. From the anthropological point of view, it makes little sense to speak of reason as a fundamental faculty that distinguishes humans from non-human beings. Rather, reason becomes one of the many customs or habits of particular peoples living together in particular places at particular times. According to Krannawitter, "instead of pursuing the truth about man and how he ought to live, anthropology, and its multicultural disciples, assume that reason is incapable of telling us how man ought to live, because reason itself is but an invention of different cultures."[134] As evidence modern philosophers trot out various examples of the many disagreements between different cultures about basic moral and political questions. From this multiplicity of perspectives, they conclude, there is no objective ground upon which we might judge or rank the many cultures of the earth. The bottom line is that "values" of each culture are equally valid compared to the values of any other culture.

The intellectual basis of multiculturalism emphasizes "diversity" and "non-judgmental approach": Since there are many interpretations of right and wrong, the only thing we can know is that we cannot know true good from true evil. Therefore, it is morally wrong to think we can objectively distinguish good civilized peoples from bad barbarian peoples. Nonetheless, certain incongruence was found within multicultural society. On one hand, multiculturalism is a product of a single culture, notably Western society, and it is not mirrored in any other major world culture. Nowhere else, from tribal

---

[134] Ibid.

Africa, the Balkans, Islamic countries, to Communist China is there any consolidated demand for multicultural "diversity." The paradox is multiculturalism itself is not multicultural in nature. On the other hand, multiculturalism builds upon the denial of universal human nature, which propounds its own survival to universal equanimity. Also it appeals unwittingly to something *true* about the human world, yet it is founded upon the denial that objective truth is possible. Krannawitter sees "in its celebration of the diversity of cultural perspectives—and in its denial of any objective or true point of view—multiculturalism becomes just another perspective. That is, on its own ground, multiculturalism cannot defend itself as any truer than non-multicultural perspectives."[135] Embracing the waves of modern philosophy that swept across America at the time, the French attempted in 1789 something never before attempted: through a so-called revolution they founded a nation upon a self-evident truth, a truth bound up in "equality, brotherhood and liberty." The new nation was conceived in liberty and heralded that all men are created equal. This proposition has been the single greatest cause of the wave of revolutions against monarchies across Europe in the 19th century. The entire European experiment of free and democratic government stood on the principle of equality, that is, citizens are equal before the law and have the same civil rights and duties within the same set of values and under a single flag. Under the influence of multiculturalism, however, the citizens were induced to discard their loyalty to the Fatherland, in the name of "diversity," and to abandon anything that tastes of patriotism. Some multiculturalists try to square patriotism with their multiculturalism by arguing that what unites Europeans is their diversity. But the conclusion

---

[135] Ibid.

of this argument is unsustainable. Individual rights, religious and civil liberty and the rule of law are either good, or they are not; a nation cannot affirm both simultaneously. If Europe stands for everything, it can stand for nothing.

Since the attack on the twin towers in 2001 public opinion in Europe has been more careful in embracing multicultural-ism, especially towards those who openly refuted Western civilization to the extent of defining it as evil. Such change in the public opinion was reflected in the following elections across Europe, where mostly center right governments pre-vailed. Consequently, the political support for multicultural-ism began to fade away. As reported by Sabine Siebold on October 17, 2010, German Chancellor Angela Merkel told a meeting of younger members of her conservative Christian Democratic Union (CDU) party at Potsdam near Berlin that attempts to build a multicultural society in Germany had "utterly failed," stating: "The concept that we are now living side by side and are happy about it does not work."[136] She continued to say that immigrants should integrate and adopt Germany's culture and values. This has added to a growing debate within Germany on the levels of immigration, its effect on Germany and the degree to which Muslim immigrants have integrated into German society.

Since the late 1990s, in Holland, the legal philosopher Paul Cliteur attacked multiculturalism in his book *The Philosophy of Human Rights.*[137] Cliteur rejected all political correctness on the issue: Western culture, the Rechtsstaat (rule of law) and human rights are the product of the Enlightenment, which is proper of Europe. Cliteur saw non-Western cultures not only different but as anachronistic as multiculturalism primarily

---

[136] Merkel says German multiculturalism has failed, Sabine Siebold, *Reuters, Sun* Oct 17, 2010
[137] Paul Cliteur. *De filosofie van mensenrechten.* Nijmegen 1999

is an unacceptable ideology of cultural relativism, which would lead to acceptance of barbaric practices, including those brought to the Western World by immigrants; inter alia: infanticide, torture, slavery, oppression of women, homophobia, racism, anti-Semitism, gangs, female genital cutting, discrimination by immigrants, suttee, and the death penalty. In 2000, Paul Scheffer—a member of the PvdA (Labour Party) and professor of urban studies—published his essay "The multicultural tragedy," an essay critical of both immigration and multiculturalism. Scheffer is a committed supporter of the nation-state, assuming that homogeneity and integration are necessary for a society: the presence of immigrants undermines this. A society does have a finite "absorptive capacity" for those from other cultures, he says, but this has been exceeded in the Netherlands. Specifically:

- A huge influx of people from diverse cultural backgrounds, in combination with multiculturalism, resulted in spontaneous ethnic segregation.

- The Netherlands must take its own language, culture and history seriously, and immigrants must learn this language, culture and history.

- Multiculturalism and immigration led to adaptation problems such as school drop-out, unemployment and high crime rates.

- A society that does not respect itself (its Dutch national identity) also has no value for immigrants.

- Multicultural policy ignored Dutch language acquisition, which should be a priority in education.

- Islam has not yet reformed itself and does not accept the separation of church and state. Some Muslims did not accept the law in Amsterdam because its mayor was Jewish.

Society may sometimes not be as ideal and equal as one would expect. As Norman Podhoretz recently wrote, "there has always been an unspoken truth about migration everywhere in the world: 'immigrants must always lose their own culture—that is the price of immigration, a brutal bargain.'"[138] His essay had a great impact and led to what became known as the "integration debate." As in the essay, this was not simply about multiculturalism, but about immigration, Islam, the national identity and national unity. The Dutch language is the language of the constitution, and therefore it must be the only public language—all others must be limited to the private sphere. "The Netherlands, he wrote, had been taken hostage by the left-wing multiculturalists, and their policy was in turn determined by the Islamic conservatives."[139] In 2004 there were 800,000 Muslims in the country, with 450 mosques.

The UK is an even clearer case of failure of multicultural society. With considerable migration after the Second World War making the UK an increasingly ethnically and racially diverse state, race relations policies have been developed that broadly reflect the principles of multiculturalism, although there is no official national commitment to the concept. It has been argued that the UK government has since 2001 moved away from policy characterized by multiculturalism and towards the assimilation of minority communities. Opposition has grown to state-sponsored multicultural policies, with some believing that it has been a costly failure. Critics of the policy come from many parts of British society. There is

---

[138] Norman Podhoretz, Current Trends in Islamist Ideology, Volume 11, Hudson Institute, 2011.
[139] Ibid.

now a debate in the UK over whether explicit multiculturalism and "social cohesion and inclusion" are in fact mutually exclusive. In the wake of the July 7, 2005 bombings, David Davis, the opposition Conservative shadow home secretary, called on the government "to scrap its 'outdated' policy of multiculturalism." The British columnist Leo McKinstry said of multiculturalism, "Britain is now governed by a suicide cult bent on wiping out any last vestige of nationhood" and called it a "profoundly disturbing social experiment."[140] Whilst minority cultures are allowed to remain distinct, British culture and traditions are sometimes perceived as exclusive and adapted accordingly, often without the consent of the local population, for example the religious holidays called with civil names, e.g., winter break instead of Christmas holiday. In November 2006, Prime Minister Tony Blair stated that Britain has certain "essential values" and that these are a "duty." He did not reject multiculturalism outright, but he included British heritage among the essential values: "When it comes to our essential values—belief in democracy, the rule of law, tolerance, equal treatment for all, respect for this country and its shared heritage—then that is where we come together, it is what we hold in common."[141] Renewed controversy sparked when Andrew Neather—a former advisor to Jack Straw, Tony Blair and David Blunkett—claimed that Labour ministers had a hidden agenda in allowing mass immigration into Britain, to "change the face of Britain forever." Tom Whitehead reported that according to Neather, who was present at closed meetings in 2000, a secret government report called for mass immigration to change Britain's cultural make-up, and that

---

[140] How the Government has declared war on white English people, By Leo McKinstry, Express Co UK, 9 August 2007

[141] Conform to our society, says PM, BBC, on December 8, 2006, at http://news.bbc.co.uk/2/hi/uk_news/politics/6219626.stm

"mass immigration was the way that the government was going to make the UK truly multicultural." Neather went on to say that "the policy was intended—even if this wasn't its main purpose—to rub the right's nose in diversity and render their arguments out of date."[142] This was later affirmed after a request through the freedom of information act secured access to the full version of a 2000 government report on immigration that had been heavily edited on a previous release. The Conservative party demanded an independent inquiry into the issue and alleged that the document showed that Labour had overseen a deliberate open-door policy on immigration to boost multi-culturalism for political ends. On February 5, 2011 BBC News reported that Prime Minister David Cameron stated that the "doctrine of state multiculturalism (promoted by the previous Labour government) has failed and will no longer be state policy; the UK needed a stronger national identity and signaled a tougher stance on groups promoting Islamist extremism."[143]

In conclusion, historic and social evidence show that multicultural society is hardly possible nor desirable for Europe, notably when tolerance is faced with intolerance and acceptance translates into the relinquishing of its own identity.

---

[142] Article "Labour" wanted mass immigration to make UK more multicultural, says former advisor, Tom Whitehead, The Telegraph, Oct 23, 2009

[143] State multiculturalism has failed, says David Cameron, February 5, 2011, BBC News

The birth of Eurabia

"Europe is no longer Europe, it is Eurabia, a
colony of Islam, where the Islamic invasion
does not proceed only in a physical sense,
but also in a mental and cultural sense."
— ORIANA FALLACI

THE ISLAMIC TAKEOVER OF EUROPE will depend on the relative proportion of Muslims compared with non-Muslims, and the influence of militant Muslims among the Muslim population. A higher proportion of Muslims among the population and the growth of militants among Muslims, drive the political development along a certain path of tense relations. Only through a successful assimilation and integration process may the tension be mitigated. Unfortunately, that path is still unchartered and no successful examples of such a process are yet available in Europe. Various social and political theories attempt to define the possible political development of a growing active Muslim community and its impact on the hosting country. According to author Noh Sharia, based on examples from countries like France, U.K. or Germany, which have been experiencing such a situation since the early '60s, "a model theory (concentrating on parts of the conflict between political traditional Islam and domestic non-Muslim forces) may be extrapolated."[144] On the basis of this extrapolation, we can then formulate the structure of a society we can call Eurabia—as already defined by Bat Ye'or in the '90s.[145] The emergence of Eurabia follows a process pattern that needs to be clearly identified and anticipated, so as to allow the development of a model that can halt and reverse this process. Such a model however needs to be integrated with accompanying policies aimed at preserving the traditional values of European societies.

The process of Islamization—or Eurabization—seems to follow a pattern where a number of phases can be identified. An underlying assumption is that a Muslim minority allows radical Islamists to influence a growing part of its population in the hosting country. "The contents of the traditional Islamic doctrine that is recognized by all major schools of Islam to be the valid one (various interpretations differ—of course—between them), seems to support the interpretations of the radical Islamists regarding many matters," says Noh Sharia. Probably a main reason for the passivity and silence of the so-called "moderate" Muslims is the fact that they who don't have a comprehensive alternate doctrine to lean upon. It is also true that most "moderate" Islamists do not openly oppose radical Islam for fear of violent reprisals. Undoubtedly, radical Islam benefits from a strong international support, notably financial support from Islamic nations and borderline organizations close to international terrorism. For decades Europe coveted an enlarged vision of the anti-American Gaullist policy based on the setting up of a Euro-Arabic Mediterranean rim resilient to American

---

[144] "Islamization of Europe and Policies to Prevent It," by Noh Sharia, January 7, 2007, IslamWatch.org

[145] *Eurabia: The Euro-Arab Axis,* Bat Ye'or, Madison, TeaneckFairleigh Dickinson University Press, 2005

influence and penetration. Such vision leveraged European ambitions to play a defining political role in international relations in competition with the United States independent of its influence. In particular, Europe maintained important spheres of influence in the former European Arab colonies with a view to open vast markets for European products in the Arab world, especially in oil-producing countries. With the goal to secure supplies of petroleum and natural gas, Europe readily endorsed the EU Mediterranean policy, aiming at a single Mediterranean economic market with zero barriers, free movement of goods and ultimately legal migration of workers. Some writers see a hidden agenda "to develop a powerful Islam-Christian symbiosis orienting Europe toward Islam, thus liberating Christianity from Judaism and its economic, political influence."[146]

In order to attain these ambitions Europe must operate under one single foreign policy as one entity. This may explain the hasty creation of a common European External Action Service (EEAS) in 2010 based on the new European Union Treaty. Each Member State would relinquish an important part of its foreign policies in favor of an EU single foreign policy forged by the EEAS. It is not by chance that France was a driving force behind the creation of the European External Service, which had "already been envisaged by General de Gaulle's inner circle and Arab politicians, including the former Mufti of Jerusalem and Nazi-collaborator, Haj Amin al-Husseini."[147]

According to Bat Ye'or, this little known legacy starts in the 1960s, when "nostalgic fascist groups began strengthening ties with Arab countries engaged in bellicose actions against

---

[146] Ibid.
[147] "Eurabia and Euro-Arab Antisemitism," article by Bat Ye'or, April 5, 2004, www.frontpagemag.com

Israel."[148] This pan-European and anti-American movement formed the nucleus of a European solidarity with Palestinian Arabs that became more assertive after 1967.

The 1973 oil crisis gave France and Germany a pretext to base the integrated Euro-Arab policy on the danger of an energy shortage, which in the views of Bat Ye'or was "used to 1) forge a shared European energy policy on petroleum and 2) cement the European Community's alliance with the Arab League countries in a common anti-American, anti-Israeli policy."[149] Thus, the French-German duo used the 1973 oil crisis to justify their political reversal. This event generated the most tangible and immediate consequence of this alliance between the European Community countries and the Arab League.

In exchange for economic stability, the Arab States demanded from Europe a few but clear political stands, notably: neutrality, vis a vis their anti-Israeli policy; modernization of their countries, particularly infrastructures and education; access to Western science and technology, especially the military; and measures favorable to Arab immigration and dissemination of Arab and Islamic culture in Europe.

Commitments between the two parties were made with the Déclaration des Neuf sur le Moyen-Orient on November 6, 1973 in Brussels and the Summit of the Arab conference in Algeria for the Arab party on November 28, 1973. As Bat Ye'or put it, "For the first time the European Nine adopted the French interpretation of UN Resolution 242 as establishing Israel's borders on the 1949 armistice line, and including Palestinian rights in all Middle East peace negotiations."[150]

These points were confirmed by the Déclaration des Neuf in London in 1977 and that same year at the UN in New York

---

[148] Ibid.
[149] Ibid.
[150] Ibid.

by the president in exercise of the Council of Europe, Henri Simonet, and again in the Venice Declaration in 1980.

Clearly, a project that was so compromising for Europe could not be set forth in written documents and treaties; the Europeans chose the formula of "dialogue." An institutional structure was devised to study all relevant questions, give directives and design programs. All meetings, committees and working groups included representatives from European Community nations and the European Council along with members from Arab countries and the Arab League. Proceedings and decisions took place in closed sessions, with no official minutes. Sessions were jointly directed by two presidents, one European and the other Arab. Bat Ye'or stigmatised that "this complicated structure implemented a policy of Euro-Arab association defined at the highest levels by the European Community and member States, hidden behind the inoffensive name, 'Dialogue.'"[151]

The Euro-Arab Dialogue (EAD) is a political, economic, and cultural institution designed to ensure perfect cohesion between the two parties. Its structure was set up at the Conferences in Copenhagen (December 15, 1973), and Paris (July 31, 1974).[152] The principal agent of this policy was the European Parliamentary Association for Euro-Arab Cooperation, founded in 1974. "The Association, which represents several hundred parliamentarians from all European parties, works to promote Arab interests and demands within each European party and Parliament, and in the European Council. The Association pressured European governments to adopt measures for economic and diplomatic pressure on

---

[151] http://en.wikipedia.org/wiki/Euro-Arab_Dialogue
[152] Ibid.

Israel."[153] It is a powerful instrument of Arabic lobbying against Israel. The other principal organizations of the Dialogue are the MEDEA Institute, the European Institute of Research on Mediterranean and Euro-Arab Cooperation created in 1995 with the backing of the European Commission, namely the MEDEA program that manages substantial European funds allocated to Arab countries.[154]

The cultural committees formed Euro-Arab associations between universities, students, publishers and media syndicates including the press, television, radio, the arts, cinema and NGOs. Exchange programs were organized for students and professors. At various symposia—like the Symposium of Venice (1977) or the Hamburg Symposium (1983)—decisions were made to promote the study and dissemination of Islam and the Arab language and civilization in European schools, universities and Euro-Arab cultural centers established throughout Europe. "At the opening session in the Venice University's great audience hall in Cà Dolphin," says Bat Ye'or, "several personalities gave welcome speeches—including Ambassador Cesare Regard, the Italian representative to the European Group of coordination for the Euro-Arab Dialogue."[155] The participants in this Seminar unanimously forwarded recommendations for consideration by the governments of the Member States of the European Community and the League of Arab States, including:

> ◦ Coordination of the efforts made by the Mediterranean
>   countries to spread the Arabic language and culture in

---

[153] "European Fears f of the Gathering Jihad," article by Bat Ye'or, February 21, 2003 FrontPageMagazine.com. See: http://www.islamreview.com/articles/europeanfears .html
[154] See: http://www.eeas.europa.eu/euromed/index_en.htm
[155] *Eurabia The Euro-Arab Axis,* Bat Ye'or, Madison, TeaneckFairleigh Dickinson University Press, 2005

Europe, through cooperation among the Arab institutions that operate in this field.

- Creation of joint Euro-Arab Cultural Centers in European capitals that will undertake the diffusion of the Arabic language and culture.

- Encouragement of European institutions either at university level or other levels that are concerned with the teaching of the Arabic language and the diffusion of Arabic and Islamic culture.

- Support of joint projects for cooperation between European and Arab institutions in the field of linguistic research and the teaching of the Arabic language to Europeans.

- Supplying European institutions and universities with Arab teachers specialized in teaching Arabic to Europeans.

- Emphasizing Arab-Islamic culture and contemporary Arab issues.

- Cooperation between European and Arab specialists in order to present an objective picture of Arab-Islamic civilization to attract students to Islamic and Arabic studies.

In May 2008 the third meeting of Euro-Med Ministers of Culture took place in Greece under the Slovenian Presidency. At the meeting, the Ministers of Culture of the Euro-Mediterranean Partnership decided to launch a process leading to the development of a Euro-Mediterranean Strategy on Culture. For the first time, the need for a coherent strategic vision was expressed and a mandate was given at the political level for the preparation of a regional Strategy on Culture. With the objective to draft a demand-driven strategy responding to the needs of the cultural field in partner countries, the EC commissioned a report to identify strategic areas for both the public authorities and the civil society.[156] A team of experts worked on a document that suggested as priorities the need for multicultural society and integration on both sides of the Mediterranean. The results of this work were endorsed in a meeting with civil society representatives from Mediterranean partner countries in Brussels on October 8, 2009.[157]

Arab and Islamic propaganda, barely disguised in academic and cultural packaging, was disseminated by organs of the EAD operating under the highest State authorities and imposed in universities, the press and cultural centers. Dissidents, whether in religious, political or cultural circles, were marginalized or reduced to silence. These measures accompanied the influx of Arab immigration whose access to Europe was facilitated in order to boost economic growth in the continent.

The process of Islamization follows a pattern with distinctive phases, which in the past tamed primarily Muslim countries. According to Noh Sharia, "in the coming years, a similar process will attain a number of European countries."[158] This process may be described as the Eurabization of Western society.

The starting block is the "typical Western society with social peace, satisfactory economic growth, ordinary crime levels and changes in government depending on democratic

---

[156]   See: http://www.eeas.europa.eu/euromed/docs/culture_concl_0508_en.pdf
[157]   See: http://www.eeas.europa.eu/euromed/social/social_en.htm
[158]   "Islamization of Europe and Policies to Prevent It," by Noh Sharia, January 7, 2007, IslamWatch.org

elections." The number of Muslims in the population is very low, and their influence on society negligible. Current examples may be Finland and Baltic states.

According to Noh Sharia, the next phase starts "when the proportion of Muslims grows but it is fairly small and contained to certain areas with immigrant population." These are generally ignored by authorities, allowing internal issues to be solved according to the prevailing culture: occasional concealed honor murders enforce internal behavior of the Muslim minority. "Timid proposals aiming at establishing Sh'aria on social matters such as recognition of Muslim holidays."[159] Current examples are the USA, Sweden, Norway and Denmark.

Preparations of Jihad: Beginning of geographic "no-go areas for the police and public administration officials. Frequent physical attacks and even single infrequent murders of policemen or persons opposing political Islam."[160] Death threats against adversaries are common. An increasing physical destruction of property by groups, influenced by the radical imams and the Jihadists. Besides frequent proposals to introduce Sharia laws, we find established "private" Sharia courts in certain areas judging matters of special interest to Muslims. "Property crimes of various types in order to finance the beginning of a domestic Jihad movement." Current examples: France; beginning in England, Holland.

In the view of Noh Sharia, the start of Jihad coincides with the "murders of individual policemen or active anti-Muslims with a certain frequency, which murders carry an evident political message. An organized countrywide Islamist movement appears, and some mosques start to retreat from liberal versions of Islam used as a deception during the initial

---

[159] Ibid.
[160] Ibid.

phases."[161] Establishment of definite no-go areas where militants put taxes on corporations and individuals. Extortion of individuals outside these areas. Frequent use of unofficial (or now maybe even official) Sharia courts as a substitute for ordinary courts, in the "liberated" areas. Militias start to form among non-Muslim groups in society. Nationalistic non-Jihad parties grow rapidly in importance in the political life. The emigration of European citizens from the country increases significantly. Current examples: Beginning in France and Belgium.

Development of Jihad: "Frequent murders of policemen, teachers and well-known individuals opposing political Islam. Physical fights between groups of Islamists and policemen, and even occasional firefights around and outside the borders of the 'liberated areas.' Militants start to openly show weapons and declare far-reaching political goals e g taking over a region or the whole country."[162] The liberal Western versions of Islam disappear completely at many mosques when it now is of less interest to Islamists to deceive, and radicals put pressure on still moderate mosques. Militias of non-Muslim groups grow in strength and start to take infrequent part in the fighting. A growing physical separation between different religious groups in the society. The level of emigration starts to become a national problem. Passive governments and passive political parties are replaced by hard-line nationalistic parties. Current example: South of Thailand

The final stage of Jihad, according to Noh Sharia is "Insurgency and the use of the state's military force against larger groups of Islamists in regular military fights. A national Home Guard is organized to try to prevent private militias

---

[161] Ibid.
[162] Ibid.

to grow and take over the main responsibility of protecting domestic citizens."[163] Campaigns by the Islamic movement to convince media and the population of their right to dominate certain areas of the country proclaimed to be Muslim. Constant murders and kidnappings of opponents and well-known persons. Coercion of Muslim young men to take part in Jihad. Regular taxation of people in the liberated areas and extortion against citizens outside those areas. Few Muslim groups help the government, while some declare neutrality. Current example: The Philippines

Finally the country is swept by civil war. "Large-scale military fights when the domestic forces fight the Islamic movement's goal to dominate a geographic region, or the country. Militias and the national Home Guard complement the army. Widespread executions, terror, cruelty, mayhem and widespread destruction reign in urban areas. Definite separation between Muslims and non-Muslims leads to large-scale movements of the population."[164] Neighboring countries may be in some cases asked by the government of the country to intervene militarily to help in the fight. Example: Lebanon.

The possible victory for Islam will allow all the new governments to enact the constitutional reforms to percolate Sharia laws into the civil code. "Traditional Islam will overtake for all more moderate versions of Islam that may exist in the country by imposing its stronger theological basis and the real doctrine. Massive and nationwide expropriations, subsidiary condition of women, conversion of non-Christians and Christians and marginalization of moderate Muslims. The new constitution will introduce the Islamic republic with only formal democratic institutions, such as

---

[163] Ibid.
[164] Ibid.

the assembly and judicial system."[165] The Islamic code will be embedded in the penal and civil code. The institution of "dhimmitude" is introduced and will regulate the life of the non-Muslims—i.e., primarily Christians and Jews. The other non-Muslim minorities will gradually be repatriated once their contractual arrangements expire. The country will experience a significant decline in the gross domestic product to be followed by a slow recovery and limited economic growth. Examples: Iran

The model proposed by Noh Sharia is quite extreme; however it well depicts a possible scenario in Europe over the next couple of decades, more so possible if the current economic crisis in Europe turns to recession in the coming years. If Europe in the coming years will show an unwillingness to protect its European citizens from the inroads of Islamists, this will lead to violent conflicts between the traditional, right wing factions and the radical Islamic movement. It seems highly possible that the development of Jihad may last long in societies with strong democratic traditions, a good educational system and a fairly homogenous ethnic population. The infiltration and dissemination of political Islam's values among non-Muslims and moderate Muslims will be carried out mainly with non-violent means. The methods of this missionary work will be structured according to principles laid down by, e.g., the Muslim Brotherhood for the expansion of political Islam in European countries.

The acceptance of the growth of Islamic influence by the majority will be dependent on how far a society has allowed violent conflict between the population groups. Liberal Democratic and left-wing governments may choose to slide down the slope toward more and more tolerance, in

---

[165] Ibid.

the name of social liberties and freedom of expression by the few; the equation being: better more freedom and less security than the contrary. However, sooner or later confronted by the continuous expansion of radical Islamic demands and actions, European voters will turn their political preferences to radical nationalistic parties. It is a sign of real weakness if traditional political parties are not able to handle the new danger correctly. If they don't and new political forces get into power, protective measures will be realized in those countries. The policy measures will eliminate the possibility of a non-integrated Muslim population group to take over and dominate the country politically and religiously.

Strictly enforced policies in favor of order and integration should build on security and preservation of civil rights as a baseline for democratic rule. The main question is when to change the approach to tolerance. Noh Sharia believes that "Considerable civil strife—perhaps even an insurgency—will happen before appropriate policy measures are taken."[166] We believe that appropriate policies should timely halt the development towards greater influence of traditional Islam, leading to violence, insurgency and, eventually, Jihad and civil war. Were Muslims allowed to become a majority in Europe, the national parliaments as well as the European parliament will reflect the new preferences of the electorate and consequently change in priorities for social and economic development. In fact the European Parliament is the most influential institution, affecting the whole EU with its legislation. Such a change may break the bond of trust between the minority of citizens—at this point non-Muslim—and their representative bodies. The original Europeans will perceive the loss of civil liberties with the risk of insurgency and riots—much like it is

---

[166] Ibid.

happening in Egypt between the Copts and Muslims in the so-called Arab Spring of 2011. The government will take no stand against radical Islam, and the police force will then be paralyzed. The fighting will be carried out by militias backed by regular troops, as it happened for decades in Lebanon.

It is useful to remember that no more than 70 years ago, in the heart of Europe, the National Socialist movement took power through regular elections and the democratic vote of the majority of its people. Once in power the Nazi government began to restrict civil liberties and abolish liberal legislation, burning the parliament building—the Reichstag—and turning in a couple of years the Republic into a dictatorship. During this process neither the police nor the courts intervened to protect the constitutional rights of the citizens—quite the contrary. To avoid the repeating of these circumstances with an Islamist majority government, civil resistance may erupt, and Muslims and non-Muslims in different European countries will join the fight on their respective sides. Given the threat of such a violent clash of cultures, the question is: how to prevent religious riots and civil wars in Europe whilst preserving civil liberties and freedom of expression? The answer naturally lies in the number of immigrants from Muslim countries, and their successful integration or assimilation in the Western way of life. Immigration in Europe should be dependent on the migrant willingness to assimilate and participate in the values and principles of Europe. To this end appropriate test and probationary periods should be introduced for legal immigration. No values that are hostile to the European society should be tolerated. However, the multicultural policies in European countries cause failures regarding integration, and Europe is left with large unassimilated groups of sometimes angry and resentful people who don't understand and/or accept European values. Integration is therefore the key to a peaceful future in Europe. If integration does not happen naturally, it must be enforced by the authorities. Integration means the a-priori full acceptance of the Western way of life—including all civil rights and duties—by all immigrants. Parallel societies inside Europe must not be accepted. Those immigrants who refuse integration in Western society cannot be accepted in Europe and shall be returned to the country of origin or, where that would be impossible, reasonable but decisive actions have to be taken in order to promote stability and internal security. If dissenting cultures are mitigated to a manageable minority, integration could be more easily achieved. Last, there should be a strict scrutiny of any public funding for teaching home languages and promoting home culture—including madrassas—in Europe. Strong cultural and religious ties with the mother country should be closely monitored and where necessary severed.

Policies to regulate immigration can only be addressed at the continental level and can therefore only be addressed by the European Union with adequate resources and response mechanisms. Europe, however, remained silent for many years. Only in the late 1980s did Europe start a foreign policy towards the Mediterranean region, which culminated with the Barcelona Conference in 1995. Moreover, only in the late 1990s did Europe address Internal Justice and Home Affairs, which dealt with immigration and integration policies across the Member States. It was very late, as Europe was already under the social and political pressure of Muslim minorities, but hopefully not too late... and better late than never.

The slow response of the European Union

"The goal of the EU is to form a region of freedom, security and justice. Freedom in this connection cannot be just the freedom of the strong, but it must be combined with fraternity and equality."
— Tarja Halonen[167]

Political will and leadership are more important than institutions.
— Jose Manuel Barroso[168]

SINCE THE END OF THE COLD WAR Europeans were convinced that the Mediterranean had become a family affair. The long-standing good relations between the northern and southern rim of the sea were looking strong and solid, and the economic prospects were encouraging. Within this context, the shared political framework of the Euro-Mediterranean Partnership (EMP) launched by Europe in the 1990s is a reflection of this conviction—notably that Europe would contribute to resolving regional political situations, including the Arab-Israeli conflict. But they were wrong: the EMP did not achieve the expected results, while changes took place that put the

---

[167] Long-standing President of the Republic of Finland
[168] President of the European Commission for two mandates, 2004–2014

Barcelona Process itself into question. In the words of Stefano Silvestri, "'The Barcelona Process did not succeed in contributing to the resolution of the Israeli-Palestinian conflict,' even if the growing perception in Europe of the threat posed by Islamic extremism brought the security objectives of the northern and southern shores of the Mediterranean closer together."[169] The Muslim countries of the southern Mediterranean rim engaged, among other things, to contain immigration towards the EU, while receiving in return substantial aid for their "democratization" and unconditional support for the stability of the Arab regimes, however authoritarian. First the war in Iraq and then Iran's nuclear ambitions, combined with the unresolved situation in Afghanistan and the risk of crisis in Pakistan, shifted the attention to the southern shores eastward, to regions in which Europe has much less influence. "The massive arrival of China and the United States in Africa opened another door to the Mediterranean—all the more so because China, India and Japan are among the biggest buyers of Gulf (including Iran) and African oil and gas."[170] While the piracy linked to the Somali crisis has reduced traffic through the Suez Channel, the traffic from the Atlantic via Morocco and the new port of Tangiers has increased enormously. Finally, French and German opposition, along with divisions over the Cyprus question, have delayed and perhaps blocked Turkey's EU adhesion process for good, increasing the distance between the European Union and the Islamic world and the Middle East. In the second half of the 2000s, the Europeans let the Barcelona Process wane and become distorted. But the stability in which they thought they could continue to live undisturbed has been overwhelmed

---

[169] "A European Strategy for Democracy, Development and Security for the Mediterranean," S. Silvestri, Istituto Affari Internazionali, Working Papers, 11 | 10—May 2011, pages 3 and 4
[170] Ibid., page 5

by the dramatic and unexpected political awakening of the
Arab peoples. Many European governments initially saw it as
a threat. When that position became untenable, with a sudden
turnaround, they embraced the revolution in Libya to the point
of military engagement. Yet, this choice merely reflects the
initial confusion: it was the result of improvisation. "Europe's
first unitary reaction was to hold an extraordinary EU summit
on March 11, 2011. It discussed a confused and underfinanced
"Partnership for democracy and shared prosperity," which
sealed the death of the old Euro-Mediterranean policy and the
Union for the Mediterranean, but did not set out any clear
strategic ambition."[171] Stefano Silvestri of the Istituto Affari
Internazionali in his working papers titled A European Strategy
for Democracy, Development and Security for the Mediterranean
writes that "the idea seems to be to extend the bilateral approach
of the Neighborhood Policy to the Mediterranean and the
Middle East, adding a dash of democratic rhetoric. If that is
the case, Europe — even though it has the most to lose — is
destined to be dragged along by the the initiatives of others".
In the same working papers he goes on to explain that in fact
Europe's External Action Service, the decision-making mechanism for foreign, security and defense policy created in 2010
as a result of the new European Treaty, has been held publicly
responsible for the uncoordinated and polemic management
of the refugee and immigrants' situation ensued in early 2011,
as debated at the European Parliament on May 10, 2011.[172]
Notwithstanding the agenda of the Euro-Mediterranean Policy,
until recently the European governments disregarded issues
related to the homeland Muslim community. On the home-
front the line was to procrastinate any concrete coercive policy

---

[171] Ibid., page 6
[172] http://www.europarl.europa.eu/RegData/seance_pleniere/compte_rendu/
traduit/2011/05-10/P7_CRE(2011)05-10_EN.pdf

on integration that may lead to friction with parts of society. However, the fast growth of the Muslim population and the ever-increasing tensions between pan-Islamic and European secular values have accelerated the political addressing of multicultural integration. It was thus discovered that thus far most studies on Muslim communities in Europe primarily focused their attention on immigration, economic and citizenship issues—assuming the minority's willingness to integrate—and ignored, by and large, all questions related to the underpinning, culturally prominent religious identity. The reason for this downplaying of the religious identity can be found in the faulty perception among social scientists: that issues of Church and State are no longer relevant to public policy. Indeed it is so in Europe, since the creation of nation states in the 19th century and the consequent separation of the secular and sacred domains. However it has not been so in other parts of the world where the nation states struggled to affirm their existence and in some cases were not a free expression of the people. Even through the first half of the 20th century, it was not unusual that a state was created regardless of its cultural and ethnic components—a clear case was Yugoslavia and is today Libya. However, C. Soper and J. Fetzer, hold that the "settlement of large numbers of Muslims in Western Europe posed a new challenge to the existing Church-State arrangements and has resurrected old religious disputes."[173] Their study appeared in the early years of the 21st century and questioned the success of the Muslim integration strategy in a number of relevant countries in Europe. The statement made by Prime Minister Cameron at the Munich conference on February 5, 2011 sums up the political failure

---

[173] J. Christopher Soper and J. Fetzer, "Religious Institutions, Church-State History and Muslim Mobilisation in Britain, France and Germany," Journal of Ethnic and Migration Studies, Vol. 33, No. 6, August, 2007: p. 934

of multiculturalism in the UK. In his speech, Cameron rejected suggestions that a change in Western foreign policy could stop the Islamic terrorist threat and that Britain needs to tackle the home-grown causes of extremist ideology. "We have failed to provide a vision of society [to young Muslims] to which they feel they want to belong," he said. "We have even tolerated segregated communities behaving in ways that run counter to our values. All this leaves some young Muslims feeling rootless. And the search for something to belong to and believe in can lead them to extremist ideology."[174] In absence of effective integration many Muslims live in so-called "parallel societies," ethnic enclaves or ghettos. "The Common Principles for the Integration of Immigrants into the EU," adopted on November 19, 2004, resulted with an increasingly more radicalized Muslim community. The integration problems entail the fact that the European Union has no one single integration model. European countries have different approaches and different national models of integration, and no one has come up with the ideal solution. Some may even argue that lack of integration with Islamic communities is a consequence of Europe's general diffidence towards clergy and its involvement in secular society. It is the legacy of the saint inquisition and strict moral education, both still well present in the European collective memory. At an institutional level, however, the European governments address the issue of integration differently. France maintains assimilation and a secular republic, promoting citizenship as a primary tool in the integration of migrants. The United Kingdom and the Netherlands promote a multicultural model, supporting liberal values and respect for cultural autonomy. Germany takes an equal stand towards

---

[174] "Cameron: My war on multiculturalism. No funding for Muslim groups that fail to back women's rights," by Oliver Wright and Jerome Taylor, the *Independent,* February 5, 2011

assimilation and multiculturalism—varying in its application from country to country—however, insisting on the rights and duties of citizenship. This significant difference between the integration strategies is explainable by the different historical, social, economical and legal frameworks of the European countries. Notwithstanding the differences, integration of Muslims must take place across Europe at local, regional and national levels. Since the late 1990s there has been a clear and present need for Europe to elaborate coherent integration strategies and to engage in cooperation with Muslim communities. However, there existed a coordination problem as the implementation of integration policy was the sole responsibility of individual Member States, rather than of the EU as a whole. To bridge this gap and offer an organic response to integration and illegal immigration, the European Union proposed a new directive that was adopted February 28, 2002 for "a comprehensive action plan to 'combat' illegal immigration and trafficking in human beings in the EU."[175] Not surprisingly, at the EU's Inter-ministerial Conference on Integration Policy, held on November 9, 2004, former Netherlands Minister for Immigration and Integration, Mrs. Rita Verdonk, stated that "Europe must not become a breeding ground for Muslim terrorism and had perhaps been too naive in previous years in ignoring the radicalization that was taking place."[176] It was easy to agree with such a statement, particularly after the murder of Theo Van Gogh in November 2004, which simply delegitimized the Dutch multicultural model of foreign integration. Since then more events, such as the Muslim protests to the published Danish cartoons in 2005, the riots of Muslim

---

[175] "Comprehensive Plan to Combat Illegal Immigration and Trafficking of Human Beings in the European Union," (2002/C 142/02), Official Journal of the European Communities, C142/23 14.6.2002
[176] Article published in the November 12, 2004 edition of "De Tijd"

immigrants in France in October 2005, and train bombings in Madrid in March 2004 and London bombings in July 2005, corroborate the general belief of a link between terrorism and Islamic fundamentalism. The historical events that have occurred in the Mediterranean Arab countries since the end of 2010 have provided a unique opportunity for the people of those countries to more freely express their wish for democracy, respect for human rights and fundamental freedoms. Unfortunately, an indirect consequence of these events has been a significant movement of populations, mainly from North African countries towards their immediate neighbors, but also towards the European Union. According to the latest estimates, more than 650,000 persons have left the territory of Libya to flee the violence there as of October 2011. These people have found hospitality in neighboring countries, primarily in Tunisia and Egypt, and many have since managed to return, or been assisted in their return, to their respective home countries. More than 60,000 migrants, mainly from Tunisia, and to a lesser extent from other African countries, have fled towards the EU, reaching the shores of Italy (most to the island of Lampedusa) and Malta, both of which suffered from strong migratory crowding pressure. In addition to displaced people and migrants, a considerable number of refugees of different nationalities, including Somalis, Eritreans and Sudanese, have left Libya, some of whom have also reached Italy and Malta. What has Europe done so far to address the migration crisis in the Mediterranean? Urgent short-term measures have already been taken to deal with the humanitarian situation in North Africa and with pressures on frontline Member States (notably Italy and Malta). So far, a total EU contribution of about €100 million has been mobilized to manage the humanitarian emergency generated by the sudden inflows of refugees and displaced persons in the countries neighboring Libya. This support has made it possible to offer temporary shelter to refugees and displaced persons and to meet their basic needs. Yet again these operations did not address the root causes of the problem: To assist illegal immigrants in returning to their countries of origin will only be a temporary solution as the same migrants will find another way to cross the Mediterranean. Estimates from the Italian Ministry of Interiors in 2008 show that only about 15% of illegal immigrants—excluding refugees—can be returned to their home countries, partly because of a lack of administrative arrangements with their country of origin, but also because many succeed in escaping the lodging facilities.[177] In February 2011, €25 million have been earmarked under the External Borders Fund and European Refugee Fund to help those Member States most exposed to the growing flows of refugees and irregular migrants with the financial consequences of these displacements, notably for Italy and Greece. The EU response to the emergency situation has been underestimated. The current migration crisis has exposed the lack of capability of the EU instrument to deal with such extreme situations and with large numbers of immigrants. Difficulties essentially relate to two categories of issues: First, the EU financial resources available for "Solidarity and Management of Migration Flows" (which includes the European Refugee Fund, the Return Fund, the Integration Fund and the Borders Fund) are not adequate to respond to all requests for assistance. In fact these funds are designed to intervene in a stable situation and not to tackle emergencies and crises. Second, the solidarity at the EU level, including the burden sharing and financial responsibility, has been less than optimal. This kind of solidarity is dependent on the will and commit-

---

[177] http://www.interno.it/mininterno/export/sites/default/it/temi/sicurezza/sottotema004.html

ment of Member States and is not very popular amongst Member States' public opinions. To address this lack of solidarity, the EU foresees a whole migration "package" to be adopted in 2012 in the areas of border control and Schengen governance, which need strengthening to prevent irregular migration, to ensure that each Member State effectively controls its own portion of the EU's external borders and to build trust in the effectiveness of the EU system of migration management. The visa policy and long-term relations with the southern Mediterranean, in particular on migration-related issues with measures to discourage irregular migration. The European Council on June 24–25, 2011, after an extensive debate, set the orientations for "the development of the EU's migration policy, as regards the governance of the Schengen area, the control of external borders, the development of partnerships with the countries of the Southern Neighbourhood and the completion of the Common European Asylum System by 2012."[178] Here again the proposed measures are excessively ambiguous and risk having a counter effect. Mobility partnership is nothing more that a politically correct branding of what is one-way immigration to the EU. In the area of legal migration and integration in the EU. Immigrants may bring economic dynamism and new ideas, filling gaps in the labor market that EU workers decline. Although this argument is questionable in its foundations and on many grounds, there is a great need for an efficient and effective organization of legal migration to the EU, such as the creation of a "Single Permit" to simplify administrative procedures for migrants. The EU must complete the Common European Asylum System by reaching agreement in 2012, on the Reception Conditions and the Asylum Procedures Directives, including a last resort emergency mechanism in

---

[178] http://register.consilium.europa.eu/pdf/en/11/st00/st00023.en11.pdf

case of exceptional pressures and a European Asylum Support Office. In the area of asylum, Europe does not yet speak with a single voice, for different national asylum policies create an uneven treatment of refugees according to the diverse bilateral agreements with third countries. In spite of its slowness, Europe has come a long way to reach a common immigration policy. The Amsterdam Treaty of 1997 created a "third pillar" for the European Union policies that addresses questions of "justice and home affairs," which in turn shall bring the EU "closer" to Europeans and become more relevant to their everyday concerns, or so it was believed. In 2002 the European Union adopted what it calls a comprehensive action plan to "combat" illegal immigration and trafficking in human beings in the EU.[179] The plan was intended to promote a more common and integrated approach to the various questions linked to these problems amongst the EU states and their neighbors. It identifies seven areas where action is urgently needed, notably visa policy, exchange and analysis of information, improved border management at the external frontiers of the EU, pre-frontier measures, readmission and return policy, Europol and the question of penalties for those engaged in trafficking or otherwise facilitating the illegal entry of irregular migrants. The Hague Program, adopted in November 2004 by the European Commission, aimed at the set-up of a common immigration and asylum policy for the all Member States, putting the main emphasis on counterterrorism and cross-border crime, and calling the EU Member States to increase mutual concern and cooperation. At the end of 2005 the EU Counter-Terrorism Strategy approved by the Council introduced four stages to

---

[179] "Proposal for a Comprehensive Plan to Combat Illegal Immigration and Trafficking of Human Beings in the European Union," (2002/C 142/02), Official Journal of the European Communities, C142/23 14.6.2002; all my citations here are to the relevant paragraph numbers

the fight against terrorism linked to immigration, namely to prevent, to protect, to pursue and to respond—that is to prevent new recruits to terrorism; better protect potential targets; pursue and investigate members of existing networks and improve capability to respond to and manage the consequences of terrorist attacks.[180] Following the Madrid attacks, a revised action plan was released by the Commission in June 2005. It sets out seven objectives; one of them is "to address the factors which contribute to, support for, and recruitment into terrorism." At the end of 2008 the European Commission presented a proposal to amend the Dublin Regulation. This proposal relates in part to the situation in which some Member States find themselves temporarily unable to cope with the intake of large groups of asylum seekers. And on April 20, 2010 the EU approved the Communication COM(2010) 171 on delivering an area of freedom, security and justice for Europe's citizens, more commonly called Implementing the Stockholm Program. The goals of the Stockholm Program regarding asylum and migration are: the creation of a single area of protection, to share responsibilities and uphold solidarity between the Member States, the achievement of solidarity with non-member countries to remove the need to seek international protection, and to further action and cooperation on combating the trafficking of human beings. On November 22, 2010, the European Commission approved the "EU Internal Security Strategy in Action: Five steps towards a more secure Europe" COM (2010) 673. The strategy identified common threats for the internal security of the EU such as terrorism, serious and organized crime, cyber-crime and cross-border crime. Last the EU issued the Communication on Migration COM(2011) 248 final on

---

[180] "The European Union Counter-Terrorism Strategy," European Council, 14469/4/05 of 30/11/2005

May 4, 2011 marking a clear stand on immigration and a milestone towards a more effective and coordinated migration policy for the coming years. With hindsight, the creation of such an area of freedom, security and justice, as proposed by the Stockholm Program, was never warmly received by the majority of the Member States. Internal security and immigration are national responsibilities and it is hard to imagine how the responsibilities on "maintenance of law and order and internal security" could be easily relinquished by national authorities. EU Member States have their own national security policies and strategies. However, it has been considered that Member States cannot respond to today's security challenges on their own, as most of these challenges are cross-border. One could say that just a state can organize and implement an internal security strategy; however the EU is developing its own. The Lisbon Treaty and the Stockholm Program have, therefore, enabled the EU to take further action in this area. The Internal Security Strategy for the European Union: "Towards a European Security Model" was only endorsed by the European Council on March 26, 2010, but it has been a major step towards effective integrated border control and European policing. The strategy identifies common threats for the internal security of the EU and calls for "an EU-wide approach" to respond to these challenges. The "Internal Security Strategy" concentrates, for the first time in one document, a European approach to internal security and attempts to define a European security model.[181] The scope of the Strategy is very broad and includes very different actors. The main aim is to strengthen cooperation as regards police, judicial, border control and civil protection matters. The ISS seeks to balance

---

[181] "The EU internal security strategy—promoting more EU integration rather than cooperation," Margarida Vasconcelos, Tuesday, March 1, 2011, http://www.europeanfoundation.org

"security, freedom and privacy." It reads: "The values and principles established in the Treaties of the Union and set out in the Charter of Fundamental Rights have inspired the EU's Internal Security Strategy: justice, freedom and security policies that are mutually reinforcing whilst respecting fundamental rights, international protection, the rule of law and privacy." The strategy puts strong emphasis on "prevention and anticipation" based on an "a proactive, intelligence-led approach."[182] It calls, therefore, for the development and improvement of "prevention mechanisms such as analytical tools or early-warning systems," with a view to enhance law enforcement through the sharing of further data. A question arises: Will the national authorities be capable of using the available data in the most effective way? This is the real challenge.

In November 2010, the European Commission adopted a Communication on an EU Internal Security Strategy Action Plan. The Action Plan proposes to focus on five objectives: organized crime, terrorism, cyber-crime, border management, and crisis management, and outlines several actions to be implemented by 2015. The document points out that "the international nature of criminal networks calls for more joint operations involving police, customs, border guards and judicial authorities in different Member States working alongside Eurojust, Europol and Office Européen de Lutte Anti-Fraude (OLAF)." The EU calls, therefore, for "more use of Joint Investigation Teams," which "should be set up—where necessary at short notice."[183] Finally, after ten years of hesitation, the EU has taken a clear direction against international

---

[182] "Internal security strategy for the European Union Towards a European Security Model," approved by the European Council on March 25 and 26, 2010, http://www.consilium.europa.eu/uedocs/cms_data/librairie/PDF/QC3010313ENC.pdf
[183] "The EU Internal Security Strategy in Action: Five steps towards a more secure Europe," Brussels, 22.11.2010, COM(2010), 673

crime and terror. It is important to bear in mind that in 2012 the EU will provide Eurojust with powers to initiate investigations. Thanks to the Lisbon Treaty, Eurojust may initiate criminal investigations and ask the competent authorities of the Member States to investigate or prosecute specific deeds and possible suspects. This allows a major takeover of the responsibilities of national public prosecutors by the European Public Prosecutor. Aiming to "cut off terrorists' access to funding and materials and follow their transactions," the European Commission will set up a Framework for freezing terrorist assets. As regards cyber-crime, in 2013 an EU cyber-crime center will be created to investigate cyber-crime and to improve international cooperation. In order to "strengthen security through border management," the EU has committed to set up EUROSUR in 2012, with the task to enforce border surveillance to stop unauthorized border crossings of illegal immigrants as well as to increase the internal security.[184] The legislation stresses the need for the police forces and intelligence services of Member States to cooperate and use new technologies such as satellite imagery to detect and track targets at the maritime border and common instruments. EUROSUR will be the instrument for sharing operational information on border surveillance and immigration at tactical, operational and strategic level. Finally the EU will make full use of the solidarity clause under Article 222 of the Treaty of the Functioning of the EU, which states that "each Member State is obliged to provide assistance to another Member State which is the object of a terrorist attack or the

---

[184] Communication of February 13, 2008 from the Commission to the European Parliament, the Council, the European Economic and Social Committee and the Committee of the Regions: Examining the creation of a European border surveillance system, (EUROSUR), COM(2008) 68 final

victim of natural or man-made disaster."[185] This new provision provides for a collective assistance between Member States and represents a step further towards an EU common defense clause. The European Commission reiterated that the Internal Security Strategy Action Plan must be based on common values including the rule of law and respect for fundamental rights as laid down in the EU Charter of Fundamental Rights. However, the Plan does not adequately reflect these values and principles in its proposed implementing actions. In fact, the Action Plan does not properly ensure a right balance between the aim of guaranteeing citizens' safety and the protection of their personal data. This can be a hampering weakness of the strategy. It will only take a judge anywhere in Europe to call for a breach in the fundamental rights of the migrant or the civil rights of a citizen, and the whole construct is drawn to a halt. As most strategies, the Action Plan implementation will show whether it will be successful or not. The real challenge will be to withstand the attacks of the civil rights militants more than the illegal immigrants' networks. Too often in the past the court has ruled in favor of preserving the civil rights of an illegal immigrant to the detriment of law enforcement or collective security. Illegal immigration is also a source of terrorist infiltration in the EU. To counter this threat, Europe launched on 30 November 2005 a Counter-Terrorism Strategy based on four pillars, namely: to prevent, to protect, to pursue and to respond.[186] For the first time particular attention has been paid to prevention of radicalization and recruitment. Nonetheless, there is no doubt that to bar radical ideologists from entering Europe or to arrest them is not enough to prevent terrorism. According

---

[185] http://eur-lex.europa.eu/LexUriServ/LexUriServ.do?uri=OJ:C:2008:115:0047:0199:en:PDF

[186] See: http://register.consilium.eu.int/pdf/en/05/st14/st14469-re04.en05.pdf

to Katrine Anspaha, at the Department of Political Science, University of Latvia, more important is "to understand the key factors and root causes of one's turning to radicalization and then to violent acts; to this end and to prevent Muslim radicalization at the very 'pre-radicalization' phase, the EU recommended the following actions"[187] within the frame of the Counter-Terrorism Strategy for Combating Radicalization and Recruitment to Terrorism:[188]

- Terrorism need be fought at both national and international levels. EU Member States should cooperate, first, at European level and second at international level between the European Union and its partners;

- By means of the common foreign and security policy instrument, the EU should expand its positive political role in the Middle East, especially, in Arab-Israeli conflict, which is one of the main causes of Muslim radicalization;

- The Member States, while upholding the principle of secularism, should respect the diversity of religions, promote social cohesion and prevent discrimination against Muslims;

- The EU governments should monitor the radicals in ways that do not risk further alienating Muslim communities;

- The EU governments should support the moderate Muslim groups and integrate them better, while avoiding a right-wing populism;

---

[187] "The Integration of Islam in Europe: Preventing the radicalization of Muslim diasporas and counterterrorism policy," Katrine Anspaha, Department of Political Science, University of Latvia presented at Fourth Pan-European Conference on EU Politics University of Latvia, Riga, Latvia, September 25–27, 2008

[188] The European Union Strategy for Combating Radicalization and Recruitment to Terrorism, 14781/1/05, Council of the EU, November 24, 2005, see at http://ec.europa.eu/home-affairs/policies/terrorism/terrorism_radicalisation_en.htm

- Concerning the institutionalization of Islam, the Europe's officials should promote the "mainstream" representation of Islam through the creation at national level of advisory representative Islamic institutions;

- The European Muslims should not rely on foreign Islamic fund organizations, rather on local European funding. The EU should monitor the funds of local mosques and Muslim organizations in order to discover the financing sources and stop terrorism financing;

- To limit radical individual or group activities in public places: in worship places (mosques), education or religious training places (schools and madrassas), prisons;

- The radical imams are posing a threat to the Muslim assimilation process into European liberal democratic society. That's why the imams should be educated and certified not in Muslim countries, but in Europe. The European governments should further the emergence of moderate "home-grown" imams and new Muslim leaders, who would protect the European Muslims from radical imam influence and Islamist terrorist group recruitment;

- It is important to pay attention to Muslim young people who are susceptible to radicalization. By discovering the motives of engaging in terrorist activities of young people, such as social exclusion and marginalization, unemployment, poverty, it becomes easier to achieve an effective anti-terrorism approach;

- To prevent individuals gaining access to terrorist training, travelling to conflict zones;

- The use of the Internet by the European Islamic extremist groups or individuals should be monitored, especially forum chats, in preventing religiously motivated Muslim immigrant radicalization.[189]

However, given that challenges have profound social, economic and political dimensions, the action plan needs to have a wider impact. Mass migrations of people, predominantly from the South to the North of the Mediterranean, has become one of the toughest challenges in Europe—contrary to the so-called new world countries like Canada, US and Australia—because the "old world" was not prepared—neither politically nor socially—to be an area of permanent immigration. Public debates have advocated in the past few years for the need of fresh "routes" of legal immigration in Europe, since the dropping demographics and skills shortages are the most frequently cited reasons. According to Sara Silvestri of the European Policy Centre, "Several EU governments—and ultimately the European Commission—have communicated a positive approach to migration, underlying the advantages of a multicultural society." Notwithstanding these efforts, "Europeans have shown the urge to secure the territory against the uninvited and the unwanted; demanding governments to police external borders intensively and tighten refugee reception procedures. In spite of these measures, observers noted the 'failure' of immigration control, such that, despite several decades of border controls, illegal immigration persists."[190] Global poverty, inequality and violence are resolved into the

---

[189] But there are also the critics of such an idea. According to one of them, this would risk deepening existing divisions between different versions of Islam, and creating hierarchies that do not exist in the tradition and history of Islam. Thus any attempt to organize these initiatives around the idea of promoting "moderate" Islam should be avoided. See Sara Silvestri, *Islam and the EU: the merits and risks of Inter-Cultural Dialogue, Policy Brief,* European Policy Centre, June 2007, p. 4.

[190] Sara Silvestri, *Islam and the EU: the merits and risks of Inter-Cultural Dialogue, Policy Brief,* European Policy Centre, June 2007

problem of "illegal immigration," where there seem to be two poles at work. The first is a cluster of malicious identities. Here we find the terrorist, the "bogus asylum-seeker," the "benefit tourist," and the "economic migrant." In certain places and at certain times even certain nationalities are sufficient to name problematic migrants and summon up suspicions, for example to evoke a "Kurd" or "Albanian" in Europe today. They are easy scapegoats for troubled societies. "Effective action against illegal immigration plays an essential part in contributing to public acceptance of admission for humanitarian grounds by preventing misuse of the asylum system."[191] The plan takes due account that, frequently, smuggling leads into trafficking. The price of smuggling services is very high, so that many illegal immigrants—when unable to pay the price—often become victims of traffickers, who employ exploitative means to gain "reimbursement" for the cost of the journey. Local organized crime plays a very important pivotal role in this ordeal, being at the same time the purveyor and customer of illegal immigrants. The counter-terrorism plan can be read as a template or a diagram for the transnational policing of mass migration, in two distinct but related senses. First, the plan defines the tasks and prerogatives of the state in relation to a problem field that is transnational, to "flows" of people and materials that traverse its territorial borders. According to Prof. W. Walters, "the transnational policing state takes as its field a space that is neither simply 'inside' or 'outside' the state, but which is transversal to it. Second, the plan is about a transnational policing state in the sense that concerns the obligations which states have to each other. The common security system is only as strong as its weakest point. Transnational policing aim is to spread networks across

---

[191] Ibid.

the existing control systems to create a seamless, extended space in which the mobility of the 'legal' is enhanced while at the same time immobilizing the 'illegal.'"[192] Ever since the Schengen agreement the vast majority of the EU states have adopted a common list of "risk" countries whose citizens require visas to enter EU territory. Other ways in which states are called upon to become more effective in policing illegal immigration include engaging in information exchange on illegal movements and organized crime, deepening networks of liaison officers across the EU, but also in problem zones (e.g., the Balkans, the Maghreb), and ensuring that all Member States adopt harsh legal penalties to punish and deter smuggling and trafficking activities in their own territories. Like any outcome of the EU policy making process, we can expect the comprehensive plan to embody and reflect power struggles between Member States—as in the recent case between Italy and France for the free cross-border movement of the 40,000 illegal immigrants from northern Africa. The plan places greater logistical demands on some states than others, notably the outer border. The next step would be to align synergetically the EU's "external policy" towards its neighboring states and home affairs policy. For instance, the attempt to organize the neighborhood policy with southeastern European states and the southern Mediterranean rim as a sort of buffer zone, insulating the EU from the main exporters of immigration. One of the core proposals of the plan is for a renewed emphasis on readmission and return since this is regarded as "an integral and vital component in the fight against illegal immigration. The disposal of unwanted population from Europe is a difficult and very expensive

---

[192] *The "Fight" against "Illegal Immigration" in Europe: Some Critical Reflections,* William Walters, Dept. Of Political Science, Carleton University, Ottawa, Canada, March 2004

process, however. Unlike the age of European colonialism, western states do not possess distant territories where they can simply transport their undesired populations. Today we are confronted with a world composed of formally sovereign states, which makes mass expulsion usually a matter to be politically negotiated. This would seem to be the primary function of the readmission agreement. Member States are urged by the Action Plan to identify without delay the third countries generating illegal immigration and negotiate and conclude new re-admission agreements with them. The EU could and should use its political weight to bring third countries that show a certain reluctance to fulfill their readmission obligations—for example Tunisia and Morocco. The readmission agreement aims at handling problem countries by imposing the obligation under international law to readmit their own nationals. To be effective the plan needs a much better integrated approach—on the part of the EU, but presumably the western powers more generally—which combines policies of development, trade, security and so on to promote conditions that may bring under control the current crisis of mass migration. However there will be continuing "flows" of unwanted people moving away from the "zones of death" and towards the "zones of life" and the problem of illegal immigration will not be solved in the near future. Particular aspects of the plan may prove successful in meeting their goals of interception, detection, deterrence, etc., but overall its prospects for success seem dim.

Is there a hidden agenda? It has become evident that policies to control unwanted immigration are almost inherently predisposed to failure. This is attributed, in part, to specific features of liberal-democratic states. For instance, the active role that human rights and their advocates have in public opinion implies that governments are legally and constitutionally constrained in their capacity to enact "crackdowns." Moreover it is almost impossible to secure national and regional-continental borders in a world where each day the border is crossed by millions of people by car, train and plane. Perhaps Europe should see illegal immigration, like delinquency, not as a sign of the failure of immigration policy and border control, but as a certain kind of perverse "success" of the contemporary regimes of power. First, and most evidently, there is the question of the economic utilization of illegal immigration. Illegal immigrants are an endless source of profit for underground and "overground" economies alike. There is, as policy experts continually remind us, a multi-billion dollar industry in smuggling people; an industry that owes its whole existence to the persistence of border controls. But beyond this, whole sectors of economic life in Europe and elsewhere are now dependent for their survival upon unregistered and undocumented low wage workers—whether as pickers in the fruit fields of southern Spain, cleaners in the offices and hotels of London or workers in the world's largest retailers in Paris. Second, we may consider the political use of illegal immigration. In Europe, the political success of various movements of the far right would be inconceivable without the presence of illegal immigrants. Whether as a scapegoat to explain the inadequacies of declining social welfare and the incidence of crime, or as an indicator for the dangers of cultural crisis, the illegal immigrant is at the heart of the political appeal of these movements. But it is, of course, not only the political extremes that today invest their political capital in the misfortunes of the illegal immigrant. As the European Comprehensive Plan suggests, this has become a fruitful policy arena for centrists and liberals as well. Illegal immigration may be regarded as a "challenge" for the European Union, but it is also an opportunity to enhance its relevance and profile with a distrustful and disinterested public. By "getting tough" with this problem, the EU hopes to prove itself relevant to the everyday lives of "its" citizens. Third, and cutting across these political and economic dimensions, we might also consider the emergence of an internal-security industrial complex. There is money to be made from the exploitation of illegal immigrants in sweatshops and orange fields, but there is also money and status to be generated in prosecuting the fight against illegal immigration. This would include the private enterprises and security agencies that manufacture human detection equipment, fences and scanners as well as large airlines that profit from the transport of deportees. This complex would also include the various public security agencies that are endowed with ever-increasing budgets by their respective governments. The past 15 years or so has seen the fight against illegal immigration, like terrorism, providing a whole class of former military, security specialists and their institutions with a renewed raison d'être. Fourth, we see specific social functions flourishing with illegal immigration, such as the social worker, the asylum counseling and generally all the NGOs that offer hospitality and nourishment to the disendowed. Illegal immigration operates within a wider economy of migration. Faced with a social climate of a widespread hostility to the idea of immigration and asylum, many European governments hold to a positive approach to multiculturalism, encouraging skilled migrants who have so much to offer to Western economy and whose "diversity" can enrich Europe. In other words, the question becomes: Does the identity of the illegal immigrant serve to bring a certain kind of intelligibility to the wider phenomenon of immigration? Is there a secret agenda behind the illegal immigration issue? Complex processes and situations can be oversimplified through easily understandable characters as if it were a play: victims, sinners, cheaters, good guys, etc. For these, and doubtless other reasons, it is not a question of failure rather successful immigration policies. For as long as a policy does not achieve its stated and often utopian goals, it succeeds in making immigration manageable. They persist, despite their "failure," because they are embedded within this much wider economy of interests, utilities and public budgets to spend. This is, perhaps, the hidden agenda that explains the long-standing failure to "fight" against illegal immigration.

Ask not what Europe can do for you...
Christian Von Rosen-Kreutz

> "Any people anywhere, being inclined and
> having the power, have the right to rise up, and
> shake off the existing government, and form a
> new one that suits them better. This is a most
> valuable—a most sacred right—a right, which
> we hope and believe, is to liberate the world."
> — ABRAHAM LINCOLN

> "And so, my fellow Americans, ask not
> what your country can do for you; ask
> what you can do for your country."
> — JOHN F. KENNEDY

*A*SK WHAT YOU CAN DO FOR *E*UROPE. We are the trustees for future generations; it is our duty to ensure that Europeans do not become a dispossessed minority in their own homeland, and it is our responsibility to ensure that Europe retains its cultural identity. Many generations of Europeans struggled against adverse conditions to create what we can today proudly call the most equitable and sustainable society on earth. We have to respect and transmit this legacy to our children ad above all we have the moral obligation to pass on the pride to be European. Europeans must retain the ability to discern Good from Evil and should never forget that some beliefs and some political systems are simply more evolved than others. Therefore, some societies and some cultures are simply better than others, they are more just, more liberal, more enlightened, and more conducive to human progress. Europe has evolved to be a good society; it is the result of "Enlightenment" and the political and intellectual revolutions that it unleashed. It took much blood and two centuries of social struggle to build Europe as is today. Europeans in general should feel proud to live in the part of the world where the average citizen lives the longest number of years in good health and in economic wealth. The idea of the equality of cultures that breeds multicultural society denies the single most critical feature of human life and human history: man's capacity of social, moral and technological progress.

What distinguishes humans from other creatures is their capacity for innovation and transformation, for making ideas and artifacts that are not simply different but better than previous generations or of other cultures. It is no coincidence the modern world has been shaped by ideas and technologies emerged from Europe's Renaissance and Enlightenment. As writer Kenan Malik puts it, "The scientific method, democracy, and universal values are palpably better concepts than those that existed previously. Not because Europeans are a superior people, but because many of the idea and philosophies that came out of the European Renaissance and Enlightenment are good."[193]

To be European means to be a free thinker while respecting other people's opinion. It means caring for a sane social

---

[193] "Against multiculturalism," by Kenan Malik, *New Humanist*, Summer 2002

and economic environment. It means being a peace seeker and a fair judge of conflicts. It mans to think before to act, striking wherever and whenever possible the right balance between cost and benefit. Europe lived two major continental wars in the 20th century that have destroyed enormous resources and killed astronomical numbers of human lives—over 50 million deaths. European means to be responsible and cautious because we have already lived and suffered the consequences of different kinds of autarchic and authoritarian societies. Amongst other reasons this is why Europe must not let neo-fascist and utterly violent cultures take over the social and political agenda. These cultures are foreign to the European culture of tolerance and appeasement. They undermine the very essence of peaceful social fabric, generating conflict and frictions at vastly popular levels. However, in spite of the past courage of Europe, European policy makers and public figures are weak and fearful. They perpetually fear loosing their privileged role in society and only truly care for re-election and reappointment. Across the continent being a politician almost always means to be corrupt or a "yes man," accommodating the requests of the wealthy and powerful to the detriment of the poor. What once was politics is now bargaining, what once were virtues are today vices. As collateral damage, the stable, shared, high standards of living in Europe are dropping fast due to economic pressure from emerging nations and the weakening of internal cohesion, notably due to excessive uncontrolled immigration.

Hence Europeans cannot expect change to start from the political institutions, for their level of involvement with the system is such that they would lose more than they would gain. After all, immigration control, integration policies and anti-terrorism is a business worth several billion Euros. It is impossible to hope that politicians have no stake in it. To bring about change citizens of Europe must act themselves, organizing pressure groups and demanding total transparency of national and European actions as well as the budget spent. Citizens have the right to know how their governments are resolving a problem that is changing the fabric of society and must demand that popular will is respected on such fundamental issues as culture and identity of Europe. The easiest trace to follow is always the money trail. Nothing can be carried out without budgets to underpin it. It suffices to verify where the public money is spent to have a clear view of the priorities of the governments. People should check the hard figures and not listen to the void promises of such compulsory liars as today's political leaders. Public money should be spent no more to support new immigrants' integration. All facilities for immigrants—including refugees—should be stopped and scrutinized by the competent authorities and committees of independent citizens. No more free lodging paid by the taxpayers' money must be provided for those who trespass the European borders. In countries with a tradition of the welfare state the situation has become socially and financially unbearable. Families of illegal immigrants are awarded allocations and lodging facilities before legal native Europeans—see Belgium, the Netherlands and Germany. At the same time the immigration flux needs to be brought to a halt. It would suffice to demonstrate the same severity with illegal immigrants as in other parts of the world. For instance, rather than lodging the migrants in hotels or other civil residences, they should be hosted in remote security camps, barracks and prisons under strict control of the policing authorities. The migrants would stay confined within these lodgings, and citizens should organize themselves to patrol the territory close to their residence until they are repatriated. Upon the failure by their countries to accept the repatriations—which is a common practice—the migrants can gain their lawful residence in Europe after 5 to 10 years of mandatory labor in socially useful projects, such as cleaning parks and streets, helping the elderly or delivering mail at minimum wage. The message here is simple and clear: Europe is open to all those hard-working migrants ready to earn acceptance. Failure to do so will imply expulsion or imprisonment. Citizens should demand from their governments that a clear stand is taken on the prevention and management of migrants and that committee of residents be allowed to see and monitor progress in this sense. Such citizens' monitoring committees could be organized by local authorities—township or province—with the participation of retired elderly, who will be happy and grateful to contribute to the security of their neighborhood. Last but not least, citizens may want to undertake the so-called European Citizens' Initiative (ECI), one of the few innovations under the Treaty of Lisbon that enables citizens to ask the European Commission to bring forward legislative proposals. Such an initiative needs the signature of one million supporters that come from seven Member States. The regulation sets out the procedures and conditions for implementing the citizens' initiative. In particular, a proposed initiative must fall within an area of EU competence and be consistent with the Union's values. Since the EU has the competence over Home Affairs, Immigration and Justice, the ECI could ask for transparency and scrutiny powers over the funding of immigration support programs, as well as popular consultative procedures for any European legislation on immigration matters. This will also serve to pass the message that policy makers cannot simply approve as they will what they deem more appropriate for Europe, without people's consent. Citizens must also ensure, in the context of illegal immigration and fake asylum seekers, that no amnesties to reward law-breakers and no extensive appeal against legal decisions be accepted. For example, the comprehensive plan to combat illegal immigration and trafficking of human beings in the European Union (Official Journal C 142 of 14.06.2002) introduced the measure of voluntary repatriation and the Communication from the Commission of June 17, 2008—"A Common Immigration Policy for Europe: Principles, actions and tools"—reinforced the instruments to assure police cooperation across Europe. However, the relevant section on funding of repatriations has been deliberately underfunded and made subject to each Member State regulation, thus becoming cumbersome and difficult to use. Europeans should ask for explanations. People should regain sovereign control of Europe's borders, asking their governments and ultimately the EU to increase infrastructure and personnel that will secure borders against intrusion, to the extent of introducing physical barriers where needed. Europe should impose a permanent lifetime ban on re-entry into Europe, enforced by instant deportation, for anyone found guilty of having violated European immigration laws. Deportation should apply to all criminal entrants, regardless of their residential status, notably Muslim extremists, regardless of their length of residence in the EU or citizenship. The European Commission should scrutinize and where necessary revoke national social engineering projects that have failed the multicultural experiment. The scrutiny should look at the cost/benefit analysis in social and economic terms. How has the project increased integration, basing the analysis over the last 10 years of output and impact indicators, such as—inter alia—the number of ethnic delinquency and crime rate, reported discriminatory incidents and convict population make-up?

Finally, Europe should start a cross-cutting review of Member States, national targets and quotas for ethnic representation in all areas of employment, public and private, including all departments and agencies of government whose specific function is to attend to the interests of ethnic minorities. A close review should also be carried out for education, notably redressing the current policies to favor racial integration in schools and reassessing the usefulness of "positive discrimination" schemes. In pursuit of liberal democratic and progressive (or leftist) globalist ideals, the European working class has been abandoned, replaced and displaced by a new ethnic electoral power base. Social and political structures should enhance and support individual freedom, equality before the law, private property and popular direct participation in decision making. History shows that no great civilization created or sustained by a multicultural population survived across time; indeed most have collapsed because they became too multicultural, with Rome and Ancient Egypt being well-known examples of this process. The fall occurred even faster in recent history: The Balkans, Rwanda, Indonesia, Ulster, Fiji, Sri Lanka and Iraq are all examples of societies losing their unity and purpose. As the British National Party 2010 manifesto explains, "Group identity, belonging, loyalty and allegiancé, in other words, are not products of 'false consciousness,' economics, imperialism or sociological processes; they are an essential part of elementary human nature. European people may take pride from knowing that the blood of a magnificent heritage of nation-building, civilization-creating heroes and heroines runs through their veins."[194] In other words, being European is more than possessing a piece of paper or a passport. It runs far deeper than that: it is to belong to a special chain of unique people who have the natural right to remain a majority in their ancestral homeland.

---

[194] http://www.general-election-2010.co.uk/bnp-manifesto-2010-general-election

The Arab Spring—what is really happening

Christian Von Rosen-Kreutz

SINCE THE WRITING OF the original piece a lot of sensational events have rocked the Arab world. Establishing a common denominator that could seriously influence Europe is at the heart of this chapter. Peaceful and well-intentioned forces are behind the dramatic Arab Spring; however infiltration from Islamic fundamentalists is a constant factor in the consolidation and export of destabilizing elements. As often mentioned, fundamentalism, no matter of which religion or political origin, is a factor that foments polarization and rapture within societies.

The series of protests and demonstrations across the Middle East and North Africa has become known as the "Arab Spring" or even sometimes as "Arab Awakening" even though not all participants in protests identify as Arab. Such awakening was sparked by the first protests occurred in Tunisia on December 18, 2010 when the martyr Mohamed

Bouazizi's self-immolated to draw the world's attention to the country economic crisis, police corruption and general poor social treatment. His act shocked the population and triggered a wave of protests across Tunisia, which affected other neighboring countries suffering from the same symptoms, notably Algeria, Jordan, Egypt and Yemen. These protests have also provoked similar unrest outside the region. In half a year, these unexpected demonstrations have changed the scenario in the Middle East, resulting in the overthrow of three heads of state: Tunisian President Zine El Abidine Ben Ali fled to Saudi Arabia on January 14, Egyptian President Hosni Mubarak resigned on February 11, 2011, after 18 days of massive protests, and last but not least, Colonel Qadhafi was overthrown after 6 months of bloody revolt officially on August 23, thereby ending the 41-year reign of Qadhafi. Other regional unrests happened that led several leaders to announce their intentions to step down at the end of their current terms. Sudanese President Omar al-Bashir announced that he would not seek re-election in 2015, as did Iraqi Prime Minister Nouri al-Maliki, whose term ends in 2014, although there have been increasingly violent demonstrations demanding his immediate resignation. Protests in Jordan have also caused the resignation of the government resulting in former Prime Minister and Ambassador to Israel Marouf al-Bakhit being appointed prime minister by King Abdullah and tasked with forming a new government. Another leader, President Ali Abdullah Saleh of Yemen, announced on April 23 that he would step down eventually.

It appears that the old military-led regimes have relinquished to a new generation of democratic rule seekers. Behind an obvious need for more freedom and democratic practices lurks the ever-present influence of fundamentalist politics. Many observers say that the spring revolts came from the common people who could not stand the oppressing regimes any longer. It was a spontaneous movement that swept across the whole Islamic nation almost in unison.

One cannot fail to notice that it was almost too well synchronized to be spontaneous: Questions arise about the true spontaneity of the uprisings and whether the majority of the citizens really desired a revolution. With a few months, hindsight, there start appearing worrisome indicators that do not necessarily point in that direction. The speculation of the first moment after the "Spring" is now being supported by hard facts and an interesting volume of studies and analytical support.

On May 27, 2011 at the G8 meeting in France, British Prime Minister, David Cameron, announced that the UK is ready to commit £110 million to help ensure the uprisings in North Africa and the Middle East succeed. According to Andrew Porter, Alex Spillius of the *Telegraph*, he said: "There is a real case for saying if you can secure greater democracy and freedom in countries like Egypt and Tunisia that is good for us back at home. That will mean less extremism, it will mean more peace and prosperity, it will mean there will not be the pressure on immigration that may otherwise face our country." Mr. Cameron added: "I want a very simple and clear message to come out of this summit, and that is that the most powerful nations on earth have come together and are saying to those in the Middle East and North Africa who want greater democracy, greater freedom, greater civil rights, we are on your side."[195] However, Britain was the only major power to commit new money to the aid package, and France and Germany declined and Italy suggested

---

[195] "Arab Spring will add to extremism if we do not help, says David Cameron." article appeared in the *Telegraph* on May 27, 2011

aid should come from key financial institutions, including the World Bank, the International Monetary Fund and the African Development Bank.

Interestingly enough, while European leaders wonder what happened and what to do next, whether unitary or scattered, other regional powers, such as Turkey and Iran, move swiftly in. Turkish Prime Minister Recep Tayyip Erdoğan undertook an "Arab Spring tour," visiting the three liberated Mediterranean countries, namely Egypt, Tunisia and Libya. On September 14, 2011, reports the *Turkish Weekly* online news, "Mr. Erdoğan made a strong statement warning Israel about the new Mediterranean balance of power. After a welcome in Cairo confirmed the Turkish strongman's soaring regional popularity, Erdoğan came to Tunisia where the wave of pro-democracy revolts sweeping the Arab world all began. 'Israel will no longer be able to do what it wants in the Mediterranean and you'll be seeing Turkish warships in this sea,' Erdoğan said after a meeting with his Tunisian counterpart Beji Caid Essebsi."[196]

Turkey was one of the first countries to support the popular uprising that started late in 2010 and in January sent Zine el Abidine Ben Ali fleeing into exile after 23 years in power. Erdoğan's visit marks "the willingness to strengthen brotherly relations and cooperation between Tunisia and Turkey,"[197] the Tunisian foreign ministry said in a statement. Ghannouchi's moderate Islamist party, which is expected to win Tunisia's first post-revolution elections on October 23, claims inspiration from Erdoğan's Justice and Development Party. "Islam and democracy are not contradictory. A Muslim can run a state

---

[196] Article appeared on the *Turkish Weekly* on September 15, 2011, see http://www .turkishweekly.net/news/123489/erdo%C3%B0an-stops-at-tunisia-for-the-arab-spring-tour.html

[197] Ibid.

very successfully,"[198] said Erdoğan, whose administration is seen by many as a model for post-revolution Arab countries. Erdoğan's popularity in the Arab world has stemmed mainly from his strong confrontations with Israel, at a time when regional leaders were seen by their people as impotent when it comes to the Jewish state and the West.

Last but not least Iran is finally making a long-awaited strong stand on the "Arab revolution." As reported on Euronews, at the inaugural international conference on the Arab Spring in Iran, delivering the opening speech, Supreme Leader Ayatollah Ali Khamenei "warned Muslim nations not to trust the US, NATO and other western nations. 'They divided your lands and looted them,' he said, 'be suspicious and don't be taken in by their smile. Behind that smile there is conspiracy and betrayal. Figures from across the Islamic world have joined senior Iranian officials, including President Mahmoud Ahmedinejad, for the conference. In terms of policy, Iran has officially supported the uprisings across the Arab world and emphasized Islam as the axis of unity.'"[199]

It seems that both the West and the East are claiming victory on the accounts of the uprising in the Arab states, although they stand on diametrically opposite positions. So we are entitled to ask, was it really a spontaneous freedom movement and if so who benefitted from it? What most matters in the short- and medium-term for the future of Europe, however, is the outcome of the ongoing pre-electoral struggles in the three geographically closest and most Westernized Arab countries, namely Tunisia, Libya and Egypt.

---

[198] Ibid.

[199] Article and video at http://www.euronews.net/2011/09/17/inaugural-arab-spring-conference-opens-in-iran/

Tunisia—The silence of the lambs

TUNISIA, THE COUNTRY WHERE the Arab Spring sparked, has been slowly fading away from the international scene, overshadowed by its more turbulent neighbor, Libya. In fact, nothing major is apparently happing in Tunisia to draw the media's attention, and that is worrying, for the Islamist always operates in silence behind the curtains until they are ready to take over power. This may result even easier in Tunisia, which has always been the most stable of all Northern African nations, with a well-developed and solid social fabric. Until January 2011 Tunisia was known as the most European country of North Africa, with a relatively large middle class, liberal social norms, broad gender equality and welcoming Mediterranean beaches. However, according to David Kirkpatrick of the *NY Times*, "in spite of its modern traits, however, Tunisia had one of the most repressive governments and levels of corruption among its elite that became intolerable once the economic crisis gripped northern Africa."[200] In January 2011 Tunisia became known as the home of the Jasmine Revolution; an explosive wave of street protests that ousted the authoritarian president,

---

[200] "Behind Tunisia Unrest, Rage Over Wealth of Ruling Family," by David D. Kirckpatrick, Published: January 13, 2011

Zine el-Abidine Ben Ali, after an iron hand ruling lasted for 23 years. On January 14, 2011, Ben Ali left the country, after trying unsuccessfully to placate the demonstrators with promises of early elections. According to the *NY Times*, "government figures issued later, 78 protesters died and 94 were injured during the demonstrations."[201] In late January 2011, the Prime Minister, Mohamed Ghannouchi, created a government of unity, bringing in members of the official opposition, to serve as an interim government until elections could be held in mid-year. But turmoil continued, with new rounds of protests and streams of alleged refugees left Tunisia for Italy—thus becoming a major cause of regional destabilization in Italy and consequently Europe. "On Feb. 27, Mr. Gannouchi resigned in response to complaints that he was too closely tied to Mr. Ben Ali."[202]

The Jasmine Revolution left a political power vacuum that has quickly been filled by the better organized political parties. Through winter 2011 the country's caretaker government was confronted with nearly daily protests by a variety of groups that destabilized the nation and further worsened the economic situation. The police force was severely weakened by mass desertions and the firing of top officials; provincial government offices remained dysfunctional. The judicial system was also hobbled by its links to the Ben Ali regime. The interim government scheduled Assembly elections for July 24, but in June 2011 it was announced that the vote would be held in October, since millions of Tunisians were still unregistered, and leaders of the dozens of new parties needed more time to be able to compete with Ennahda—the Islamic party banned by Ben Ali in the eighties. It is noteworthy that

---

[201] http://topics.nytimes.com/top/news/international/countriesandterritories/tunisia/index.html
[202] Ibid.

notwithstanding its 30-year official forbiddance, Ennahda has emerged as the better organized political party. According to the TY Times, the "June 2011 polling suggests that Ennahda—whose name means 'the Renaissance' in Arabic—enjoys broader support than any of the country's other 60-odd authorized political parties, most of which did not exist until after the revolution."[203] Accused as subversives or terrorists, members of Ennahda suffered in prison or in exile, thus gaining political credibility as a force that can break with the past, particularly among the country's rural areas. Despite repeated assurances for tolerance and moderation, Ennahda did not spare attacks on unveiled women and artists, raising fears on plots to turn the country into an Islamic republic. Ennahda's popularity and organizational strength are of growing concern to many activists and politicians among the coastal elite, who worry that the Jasmine Revolution might give birth to a conservative Islamic government in October. After Ben Ali died of a stroke in February 2011, he was convicted in absentia of theft and unlawful possession of cash and jewelry. "He and his wife were sentenced to 35 years in prison and a 65 million Euros fine."[204]

Tunisia is special in so far as it has been the first upheaval where protesters came together over social networks like Facebook and Twitter. Many were unemployed college graduates, and they angrily demanded more jobs and denounced what they called the self-enrichment of Tunisia's ruling family. It was not religion, nor the adventures of a single leader, nor wars with Israel that energized Tunisia's upheaval. It all started because of bad economic conditions and corruption by the public administration. Both these

---

[203] Ibid.
[204] Ibid.

problems have not been really addressed by the transitional government, notably due to the world's recession and the public administration resistance to change. In reality the only real outcome of the Jasmine Revolution was the peaceful invasion of the Italian coasts. Under the false pretext of humanitarian crisis and political asylum, over 70,000 young Tunisians have found their way to a better way of life in Europe. This would have been impossible under normal circumstances. The reality is, in fact, that a majority of the Tunisians fleeing to Europe know well the country's future is dim and fear the takeover of Islamist parties, which will bring a dramatic end to the liberal way of life that citizens enjoyed under Ben Ali. The irony of the situation is that the more young liberal Tunisians leave the country, the more likely is the country to fall prey to the Islamist at the next elections. In February 2011, the head of a Tunisian government commission, which is tasked with dismantling the repressive laws of the Ben Ali government, as the *NY Times* reports on June 24, 2011 "warned that the country faced a dangerous transition as it struggled toward multiparty democracy. Yadh Ben Achour, a prominent lawyer who is the head of the country's Higher Political Reform Commission, pointed to 'numerous shortcomings and deficiencies' in the organization of the election. It noted in particular that several hundreds of thousands of Tunisians don't have any, or valid, identity cards. Elections under these conditions would have warranted a clear victory of the better organised."[205] In September 2011 the political landscape counts around 105 political parties. According to Asma Ghribi of Tunisia Life, "many Tunisians are asking about their ideological

---

[205] Article on *New York Times* of June 20, 2011; http://topics.nytimes.com/top/news/international/countriesandterritories/tunisia/index.html

backgrounds and their sources of funding. Ennahda, the Islamist party, emerged as Tunisia's most generous party. Rumours circulating in the social networks claim that Ennahda is receiving financial support from Gulf countries, Qatar in particular. British media have reported that Sheikh Rached Ghannouchi, head of the Ennahda, is one of the wealthiest Arabs. Ennahda's leaders have denied all these accusations."[206] Their way for making publicity is to be generous by organizing collective marriages, and giving tiny amounts of money to people aiming at starting their own small businesses. On the other hand the Democratic Progressive Party (PDP) has opted for mobile publicity. Billboards and posters are everywhere showing Najib Chebbi, head of the PDP next to Maya Jribi, the secretary general of the party. PDP is criticized for having started his campaign of personalities too early. The Democratic Forum for Labor and Liberties (FDTL) founded by Mostfa Ben Jaafar has chosen to focus on advertising using digital big screens. The party is thought to have signed contracts with corporate advertisers and is criticized for wanting to take over people's minds. Critics state that this party's strategy considers people as consumers and not voters.[207] The National Free Party has also recently become controversial. Several questions were raised about the past of its founders and also the tremendous sources of funding that have allowed them to conduct a campaign using several media outlets. Slim Riahi, its founder, is accused of having suspicious relations with Libya and Britain, especially given that

---

[206] "Rumors Spread about Tunisian Political Parties and Their Funding," by A. Ghirbi on Tunisia Live on August 5, 2011; http://www.tunisia-live.net/2011/08/25/political-parties-in-tunisia-and-their-alleged-relations-with-foreign-countries/
[207] Ibid.

his family lived in Britain for some time before returning to Tripoli to later work on petroleum sector projects.

According to Al Jazeera International, "a survey compiled by Emrhod Consulting Institute in July 2011 showed the following: 51% of Tunisians have no idea about which party they would vote for, while the rest were divided as follows: Ennahda came first with 45.8%, PDP came second with 20.3%, PCOT came in the third place with 12.5%, Ettajdid was fourth with 11.1%, and CPR came in fifth place with 7.3%. Some new parties have started to assert their presence. For instance, the Party for Justice and Equality (PEE) got 4.5%, followed by the Socialist Left Party (PSG) with 3.2%, Progressive Unionist People's Movement (MPUP) with 3.1%, Direct Democracy Party (PDD) with 2.9%, and Al Majd with 2.2%. A poll from July 2011 (partly sponsored by Al Jazeera) showed Ennahda in the lead with 21%, with its closest rivals PDP at only 8%. PCOT was ranked third with 5% of the people supporting it."[208] In the same poll, respondents were asked to rank how strongly they identified with five political ideologies: Islamism, Arab nationalism, liberalism, communism and socialism. According to the same sources, "some 47% of the Tunisians polls said they strongly agreed with political Islam, 19% with Arab nationalism and 19% with liberalism. Only 6% felt strongly in favour of communism or socialism, respectively."[209]

Finally came the V-day in Tunisia: in the country's first free election, millions of Tunisians voted on October 24, 2011 for a general assembly to draft a constitution and shape a new government. As predicted by the polls the moderate Islamist

---

[208] "Tunisians undecided ahead of October vote, Al Jazeera," July 6 2011; http://english.aljazeera.net/news/africa/2011/07/20117617715460755.html
[209] Ibid.

party Ennahda emerged as the winner, with 41 percent of the eligible casted votes according to election officials. As reported by Allan Bradley,[210] the new assembly of 217 seats will see the following parties represented:

Party	Ennahda	CPR	Aridha Chaabia	Ettakatol	PDP
Seats	91	30	19	21	17
Party	Democratic Modernist Pole (PDM)	Afek Tounes	Mouvement Patriotes Democrates (MPD)	Al Moubadara (Initiative)	PCOT (Communist)
Seats	5	4	2	5	3

Ennahda will lead the formation of a new coalition government and name its prime minister, and it will also have the heaviest weight in the assembly on the new constitution. According to the *NY Times,* the Ennahda party has tried to "reassure secularists nervous about the prospect of Islamist rule in one of the Arab world's most liberal countries by saying it will respect women's rights and not try to impose a Muslim moral code on society."[211]

Most Tunisians are caught between a moderately Westernized past and a possible Islamist future. The majority is confused. In times of economic crisis and in the absence of a clear ideology or social model, probably Ennahada will loose its strong Islamist roots in favor of a more pluralist approach to a complex society. Yet it may resolve to take a

---

[210] "Tunisian Election Results Tables," by Allan Bradley, Tunisia Life Net, November 8, 2011

[211] http://topics.nytimes.com/top/news/international/countriesandterritories/tunisia/index.html

more denominational approach and by handing out money provided by friendly Gulf Arab states, buy its way into power, a deja-vu politics for most Tunisians.

Egypt and the Muslim Brotherhood

EVEN BEFORE THE REGION'S REVOLUTIONARY meltdowns began, according to Walid Phares, "Egypt political analysts soberly warned about the contest that would ensue between the dispersed and disorganized proponents of liberal democratic reform and the Islamists, led by the Muslim Brotherhood."[212] Indeed, as soon as the uprisings erupted on the streets of Cairo in January 2011, the Islamist political machine went into high gear. Thanks to influential backing and the support of Qatar and Turkey—notably the Adalet ve Kalkinma Partisi (AKP) (Justice and Development Party)—Egypt's Sunni Islamist movements gradually rose from the bottom and seized the initiative. At first, Islamists pursued their protest and infiltration strategy avoiding any statement or action that might associate the demonstrations with long-term Muslim Brotherhood goals. "All Islamic militants were instructed to make no mention of Shariah or the caliphate, and to target the corrupt and authoritarian regimes with no attack on the West,"[213] Public US, European and even Israeli flag burning was forbidden. Finally the Islamist movements

---

212 Walid Phares, "The Coming Revolution: Struggle for Freedom in the Middle East," Amazon.com books
213 Walid Phares, "The Coming Revolution: Struggle for Freedom in the Middle East"

pushed forward the Shabab al Thawra ("youth of revolution"), a smokescreen to camouflage their predatory intentions with the uprisings' secular, liberal democratic jargon.

While masses, and particularly young people, were exploding against Mubarak, Islamist networks were systematically infiltrating each new political movement. As long-timers infiltrated pro-democracy forces in Egypt, the Brothers are preparing for parliamentary and possible presidential elections. They launched a political party, a media campaign and a political offensive that will run into the millions. So much so, that in a reversal of a five-year-old US policy banning contact with the Muslim Brotherhood organization in Egypt, on June 30, 2011 Secretary of State Hillary Clinton announced that American diplomats will resume contact with the Islamist group. As reported by Arshad Mohammed on Reuters, "Clinton made the following statement at a news conference in Budapest, 'We believe, given the changing political landscape in Egypt, that it is in the interests of the United States to engage with all parties that are peaceful, and committed to non-violence, that intend to compete for the parliament and the presidency.'"[214] This resumption of formal contacts is a clear victory for the Brotherhood and it is also a signal to the Egyptian military that the United States has no problem with the Brotherhood's bid for more influence in the country, paving the way for a forced coexistence between the army and the Islamist party. The Obama administration hopes "democracy will change Egypt for the better and dealing with the Islamist party is just part of the price America must pay for this development."[215] However, an ideology-driven group like the Brotherhood will hardly allow itself

---

[214] See: http://www.reuters.com/article/2011/06/30/us-usa-egypt-brotherhood-idUSTRE75T0GD20110630

[215] Ibid.

to be transformed into a democratic partner. The Muslim Brotherhood only seeks to exploit Egyptian democracy to get to power and make it impossible for non-Islamists to thwart their rise to power. The Brotherhood is simply applying a well-known model in Europe, where non-democratic parties in the 1930s went to power through democratic elections—i.e., Germany and Italy. The Muslim Brotherhood has also been coaching Egypt's armed forces on regional diplomacy, opening Gaza's gates and Hamas being hosted in Cairo. Also, the Muslim Brotherhood has insinuated itself into Syria's popular uprising against that country's Ba'athist dictator. The Muslim Brotherhood in Syria has a score to settle with the Assad dynasty over the massacre of thousands of militant Brothers in the 1980s. The regional consortium of Brothers and their Salafist allies have their eyes on several other countries in the region as well, including Morocco, Algeria, Mauritania and eventually, parts of Lebanon, Iraq and Sudan. While moving with stealth and efficiency, the Muslim Brotherhood is also cleverly pausing to obviate concerns that might arise over possible Western partnerships.

In the meantime, the so-called non-Islamist democratic reformers—probably still the majority of young Arab men and women, and ethnic minorities—who bore the brunt of the violent repressive strikes, are being out-maneuvered and marginalized in the political scene by the better organised Muslim Brothers. The Brotherhood is seriously posed to become the largest political party after Egyptian elections; likely to be called to form the new government. It will probably be the last government of pluralist and democratic in Egypt and the first of a new Islamic republic. What at first seemed a massive victory of the common people may well turn out to be the beginning of a new Sunni rule in the Middle East. In fact, the recent uprisings in North Africa and the Middle East should not be viewed as an "Arab Awakening" but rather as a "Sunni Awakening." For decades, Iran has been the only state in the Middle East with a revolutionary Islamist government, as Saudi Arabia's regime is Islamist but not elected. In the past decade, the only large scale non-violent Sunni Islamists accession to power took place in Turkey. According to Zach Paikin of JINSA, "Turkey is indeed proposing itself as a reliable and powerful interlocutor not only between Europe and Asia but as alternate to Shiite Iran dominated movements. The centuries-old conflict between the Ottoman and Persian Empires may revamp as Turkey and Iran begin to compete for regional hegemony, in resurgent Arab world and looking to take the leadership role in the struggle against Israel."[216] In this context, Egypt is strategically positioned as it has a long border with Israel and a border with the Palestinian territories. The most likely scenario over the short run is Egypt undergoing a slow but steady Islamist consolidation of power, which would meet with civil society protests, while the military will be a significant independent actor, although bound by public opinion.

Amidst social turmoil and after several deadly clashes during demonstrations in Tahir Square, on November 28 Egypt will hold the first parliamentary elections of the post-Mubarack era. It will represent the next vital stage in the country's post-revolutionary history. The vote will determine who is going to control the parliament that will elect a 100-member committee that will write a new constitution. The elected parliament will also liaise with the Supreme Council of the Armed Forces, which have been ruling current affairs since February, in order to appoint a new cabinet.

---

[216] The "Arab Spring" and Its Strategic Implications for Israel, by Zach Paikin, The Sentry, Jewish Institute for National Security Affairs, September 6, 2011

According to Said Shehata of BBC news, the new parliament shall "assure government until presidential elections, which have now been brought forward to mid-2012."[217] There are more than 50 parties in Egypt; more than 30 are fielding candidates. Two-thirds of the seats are decided by party lists under a proportional system, whereas the final third are chosen through individual lists under an absolute majority system in which a candidate needs more than 50% to win a seat. If noone wins a majority, there is a second round or fearful chaos.

---

[217] Egypt elections pose daunting challenge, by Said Shehata, BBC News, November 25, 2011

The end of Qadhafi's regime

A WEAKENED OR PARTITIONED LIBYA could become a breeding ground for Jihadists engaged in a low-level insurgency against the remnants of the Qadhafi's regime, officials and analysts said, noting that Jihadists flourish mostly in failing rather than failed states. In March 2011 Reuters reporteed that "there is … the risk of division within the country and the risk of seeing a failed state in the future that could be a breeding ground of extremism and terrorism, so obviously this is a matter of concern," said NATO Secretary-General Anders Fogh Rasmussen at a NATO defense ministers meeting.[218] Libyans constituted the third-largest contingent of Jihadists in Iraq after Iraqis and Saudis. Several Libyans also graduated to senior positions in Al Qaida, including Abu Yahya al-Libi, the group's chief ideologue. The Libyan Islamic Fighting Group (LIFG), which attempted to assassinate Qadhafi on three different occasions, posed the greatest threat to the Libyan leader's regime prior to the popular revolt.

Revolution started in February 2011 almost as unexpectedly as in Tunisia, led by groups of youth and students of the Benghazi University supported by local tribe leaders. In the first phase of the conflict the rebellion was losing grounds and the loyalists started bombarding Benghazi. Just as the

---

[218] http://af.reuters.com/article/libyaNews/idAFWEA790520110310

rebel troops were about to dismantle, the NATO began its air strikes and under international pressure, Shabab al Thawra ("youth of the revolution") was recognized as the legitimate Libyan democratic force, soon to become the Liberation Government. Funded by Qatar, the Shabab managed to take a significant place inside the Interim National Council in Benghazi, particularly after the assassination of rebel military commander Abdel Fatah Younes in July 2001. Younes was the subject of much scrutiny and skepticism among anti-regime Libyans both in the country and abroad since he became the highest-profile government figure to defect to the rebels' side, on February 20, after five days of increasingly bloody protests in Benghazi and elsewhere in the country. Although the opposition National Transitional Council quickly made Younes chief of staff of the rebel armed forces, a power struggle ensued between Younes and long-time exile Khalifa Hifter, also a former general in Muammar Qadhafi's army with a more open attitude towards Islam. For much of March and April, control of the rebel army seemed to pass back and forth between Hifter and Younes. Sometimes it seemed neither was in control.[219] His departure cleared the way to Hifter as the chief in command, and with him the Shabab supporters. As it happens in Egypt, Shabab abstains from publicly declaring their ideology, or making strong statements on the future Libyan society. This low profile earned them NATO support and the European favors, including humanitarian aid and funding. But who are the rebels? What interests hide behind the names of a few leaders that until six months ago were perfectly unknown to the Western public?

---

[219] Al Jazeera, July 28, 2011; http://english.aljazeera.net/indepth/features/2011/07/2011728215485843.html

Many of the rebels are Islamist fighters who were released from prison in the past couple of years as part of the government rehabilitation program that was overseen by Qadhafi's son, Saif al-Islam, in which they repented their ways, but did not fully renounce violence. Analysts said the Jihadists' role in the struggle to topple Qadhafi would strengthen their position irrespective of what the outcome is of the battle for Libya.[220] Evidence is emerging that some Western nations including the United States forces might be waging war in Libya on behalf of rebels whose ranks include Jihadists who fought against the US in Afghanistan, Pakistan and Iraq.

Britain's *Daily Telegraph* reporters Praveen Swami, Nick Squires and Duncan Gardham, claim that "Abdel-Hakim al-Hasidi, a leader of the western-supported rebel forces in the fighting around Adjabiya, went to Afghanistan in 2002 to fight against the 'foreign invasion'—that is, US and coalition troops who invaded Afghanistan in retaliation for the September 11 attacks." The *Telegraph* says "Al-Hasidi told an Italian newspaper, *Il Sole 24 Ore*, that he was captured in 2002 in Peshawar, Pakistan."[221] Among the rebel troops are militiamen, the long-repressed Islamists, returned exiles and former Qadhafi supporters. Reconciling them might prove to be a major challenge in a country with no history of democratic rule. Qadhafi was captured in Sirte "by members of the Libyan National Liberation Army after his convoy was attacked by NATO warplanes as Sirte fell on October 20, 2011 and then killed by NLA fighters," as reported by Chris Hughes of the *Mirror*.[222] It is very possible therefore that a struggle between

---

[220] Deutsche Welle article March 26, 2011, see http://www.dw-world.de/dw/article/0,,14934994,00.html

[221] Appeared on Fox news on March 26, 2011, see http://nation.foxnews.com/libya-war/2011/03/26/shock-america-fighting-side-al-qaeda-libya#ixzz1Y2Hazwdw

[222] Confirmed Gaddafi dead: Colonel Gaddafi killed in cold blood begging for his life, by Chris Hughes, *Daily Mirror* 20/10/2011

secular and Islamist politicians will now begin. The stake will be the definition and the character of the new Libya. Even as the Transitional National Council tries to establish itself in the capital, restore Libya's oil industry and public order. According to Patrick J. McDonnell of the *Los Angeles Times,* "On September 12, a prominent Islamist scholar denounced Jibril and his allies as 'extreme secularists' who seek to enrich themselves via 'the deal of a lifetime.' Jibril and his associates were guiding the nation into 'a new era of tyranny and dictatorship.' The cleric charged that the new administration could be 'worse than Qadhafi.'"[223] In fact, the rebels' civilian administration based itself in the eastern city of Benghazi during the six-month struggle. Jibril only arrived in Tripoli in mid-September; almost three weeks after the capital fell to rebel forces. He has obliquely assailed those who put politics ahead of other pressing issues, but has refrained from direct replying to criticism of Islamists or others pushing for influence in the new state. An opponent to Jibril is Salah Mohammed Ali Abu Obah, a 43-year old Manchester, England, resident said to be a member of the Libyan Islamic Fighting Group (LIFG), an Al Qaida affiliate founded by Libyan fighters in Afghanistan. Abu Obah described himself as a low-level LIFG fundraiser. Abu Obah's statements fuelled Western concerns that Jihadists and militant Islamists were playing a key role in the Libyan revolt unlike elsewhere in the world where they have largely been relegated to the sidelines. Although Abu Obah noted that the LIFG had broken its ties to Al Qaida in 2007 around the time that its imprisoned leaders engaged in serious dialogue with the regime as part of the government's rehabilitation program. "The part of the LIFG

---

[223] Article on *Los Angeles Times,* September 13, 2001; http://articles.latimes.com/2011/sep/13/world/la-fg-libya-factions-20110914

that I am with does not belong to Al Qaida," Abu Obah said. LIFG is the only civilian group within the Libyan opposition with battle experience. The Libyan Jihadists fought a bitter insurgency in eastern Libya in the 1990s.

Another political leader in Libya is Mustafa Abdel Jalil, the country's Justice Minister until he resigned in protest over the regime's brutal treatment of peaceful demonstrators in February. Mary Fitzgerald from the *Irish Times* reports that "he stated on September 13 'We strive for a state of the law, for a state of prosperity, for a state that will have Islamic Sharia law as the main basis of legislation,' to be contained in the National Transitional Council's draft constitution.'"[224] Abdel Jalil called on Libyans to support a democratic system that honors Islam and respects the rule of law" "We will not accept any extremist ideology, on the right or the left," he warned. "We are a Muslim people, for a moderate Islam, and we will stay on this road."[225] Speaking later on Al Jazeera, Younes Abouyoub, a research scholar at Columbia University, described the speech as "extremely timely," not least because of the fissures that have begun to emerge among the rebels. He added that Abdel Jalil wanted to make sure that people understand that this revolution is not going to steer the state towards a liberal, Western-style state.[226]

Some Islamists in Libya, like their counterparts elsewhere in the region, talk approvingly of the model offered by Turkey's ruling AKP, a party with Islamist roots. "The goal, for which the Libyan people have sacrificed so much, including their blood, is to have democracy, justice, freedom

---

[224] Mary Fitzgerald, *Irish Times*, September 14, 2001; http://worldnewsnow.gospot .info/tag/ali-salabi/

[225] Ibid.

[226] Article on Al Jazeera, September 13, 2011; http://www.aljazeera.com/news/ africa/2011/09/2011912214219388500.html

and equality," Sheikh Ali Salabi, a prominent Libyan cleric often described as linked to the Muslim Brotherhood, told journalists recently.[227] "The new Turkey seems to fulfill a large part of the ambitions and hopes of most people here." Salabi used an interview on Al Jazeera to strongly criticize members of the council—including Prime Minister Mahmoud Jibril and his deputy Ali Tarhouni—as being out of touch with ordinary Libyans. Salabi also feels strongly that Islam must be an element of Libya's new constitution. He recently stated, "Islam was the fuel of this revolution, it motivated people. Islam is part of the culture in Libya and it always has to be part of the constitution."[228] Sheikh Salabi, warned of what he called "extremist secularists." Those who support him often appear wary of Western-educated Libyans who spent years living in Europe and the US and tend to be more liberal than those who stayed. Another emerging figure with Islamist background is Abdul Hakim Belhaj, a former member of the Libyan Islamic Fighting Group (LIFG), a militant organization that long opposed Qadhafi. He is now the commander of the Tripoli military council. In recent days, the group's spokesman Anis Sharif has called for Jibril to resign. Competing visions between Islamists and secularists are a worry for many Libyans. "I am concerned about the Islamists and their agenda," says Nasser, a businessman who has lived for almost two decades in the US. "I believe the Libyan soul is essentially Mediterranean and not suited to the kind of state many of them would like to see. I think this is going to be one of the biggest battles we face in the future."[229]

---

[227] Mary Fitzgerald, *Irish Times,* September 14, 2001; http://worldnewsnow.gospot.info/tag/ali-salabi/.
[228] Ibid.
[229] Ibid.

In reality, European analysts fears that many of the rehabilitated escapees may revert to their old ways. As reported by Nic Robertson on AINA, "Al-Salabi's is backed by prominent Saudi cleric Salman al-Auda, a reformed militant, and Egyptian Muslim Brotherhood spiritual leader Yousef Qaradawi. Noman Benotman, the London-based former LIFG leader who was one of the group's negotiators with Saif al-Islam, warns that eastern Libya hosts a younger, more radical group of Islamist militants who see Jihad as a religious obligation. Nonetheless, Benotman suggested that Qadhafi's pinning of the revolt against his regime on Al Qaida meant that former LIFG fighters feared that they may be targeted by the Libyan leader's forces."[230]

Opposition leaders have stressed that their revolt is nationalist rather than Islamist in nature irrespective of the fact that LIFG fighters have joined their battle. "If there's one thing you should remember, it's that this is a people's revolution, a secular revolution," said Khaled Ben Ali, a spokesman for the rebel national council. Analysts concede that the Islamists participation in the fight does not necessarily change the nature of the revolt, but cautioned that it remained to be seen whether they had truly broken with their Jihadist past. "They may no longer feel obliged to keep up their end of the bargain with a weakened government—a government many never accepted as legitimate in the first place. Violent Islamists have long sought to bring down the hated Qadhafi regime—just as they have looked to topple other 'apostate' governments in Egypt, Tunisia, Saudi Arabia, and Yemen—and some may now see this as their best opportunity to

---

[230] Assyrian International News Agency on September 2, 2011; http://www.aina.org/news/20110902164758.pdf

overthrow the government," Boucek commented according to Robertson.[231]

Libya was formally declared liberated three days after the murder of Qadhafi, that is, the October 23, 2011. This date marks the beginning of the process of setting up a new constitution and an elected government. By early November 2011, many of the local militia leaders who helped topple Colonel Qadhafi abandoned a pledge to give up their weapons. According to *NY Times* reporters A. Nossiter and K. Fahim, "they intend to preserve their autonomy and influence political decisions as 'guardians of the revolution.'"[232] The issue of the diverse militias is one of the most urgent facing Libya's new provisional government, the Transitional National Council. Since the end of the revolution there have been several clashes between militias and numerous revenge killings, many civilian leaders, along with some fighters, say the militias' shift from "merely dragging their feet about surrendering weapons to actively asserting a continuing political role poses a stark challenge to the council's fragile authority. According to Nossiter and Fahim, Human Rights Watch employee Peter Bouckaert of 'documented the killings and said the victims, who included Qadhafi loyalists and a senior official in the former government, had been found in the garden of a hotel in Surt. Several had their hands tied behind their backs. The victims were thought to have been killed about a week ago, when the hotel was a base for several former rebel brigades from Misurata, Mr. Bouckaert said.'"[233]

The *NY Times* reports, "the council has pledged in a 'constitutional declaration' that 'within eight months after

---

[231] Ibid.

[232] Revolution Won, Top Libyan Official Vows a New and More Pious State, by A. Nossiter and K. Fahim, *NYTimes*, October 23, 2011

[233] Ibid.

the selection of a new government, it will hold elections for a national assembly, which will oversee the writing of a constitution. Members voted on October 31 to name as prime minister Abdel Rahim el-Keeb, an electronics engineer and Qadhafi critic, who spent most of his career abroad."[234]

On November 19, 2011, Libyan militia fighters captured Seif al-Islam el-Kadafi, the last fugitive son and onetime heir apparent of Colonel Qadhafi, in Zintan, a western mountain town, setting off nationwide celebrations but also exposing a potential power struggle over his handling. The next day, revolutionary fighters captured Abdullah Senussi, the intelligence chief for Colonel Kadafi, in Libya's southern desert. As the prosecutor for the International Criminal Court, Luis Moreno-Ocampo arrived in Tripoli to discuss the terms of surrender and trial of the prisoners, Libya's minister of justice, "Mohammed al-Allagi, told reporters that Libya would not send Mr. Qadhafi to the international court in the Hague for trial and he will be tried in Libya."[235] This can only be interpreted as a clear sign of disrespect for international law and its institutions, probably the first of many more to follow.

On November 22, 2011, Prime Minister Abdel Rahim el-Keeb appointed the militia's commander Osama al-Juwali to be the new defense minister. The selection of al-Juwali to lead the most critical post in the government underscored the weakness of the interim government. According to the *NY Times*, the new Defense minister will now need to embark in the arduous task "to disarm and merge divergent militias from around the country into a united army and a national police force."[236] Oil executives were also heavily represented in key ministries. Abdulrahman Ben Yezza, a

---

[234] Libya—Revolution and Aftermath (2011), *NY Times*, November 22, 2011
[235] Ibid.
[236] Ibid.

former executive with the Italian oil company Eni, the biggest foreign producer in the country, will be the new oil minister. Hassan Ziglam, an executive with the national oil company, was named finance minister. The new cabinet will govern until an election for a new national assembly scheduled for mid-2012. The future of Libya is still an open game, where the local claims for democracy and political freedom are probably the least concerns. Libya is cursed by its riches: it beholds under its ground the third largest known oil reserve of the finest quality. Any world power would roll over any local politician cadaver to put his hands on such a jackpot. It is very unlikely that Libya will fall into fundamentalist hands, and even if it were, the world powers will certainly strike a deal they cannot refuse to assure the exploitation of the reserves. The example of what happened to Iraq in 2003 is too near and clear.

From a European perspective the only certainty is that no matter how the northern African states will manage the transitional periods and their new *democracies*, there will come a renewed wave of work-seeking immigrants, be it refugees or simply illegal immigrants. This never-ending immigration will put additional social and financial strain on European economies that are already reeling from decades of over lever-aging and lack of consistent growth. Recession and additional social assistance are bound to affect even more European national budgets. National studies conclude that each illegal immigrant is costing an average of eighty Euros per day to the European taxpayer. The increasing lack of work and the soaring unemployment rate will exacerbate delicate social issues that a large immigrant (legal and illegal) wave could cause across Europe and particularly in southern European nations. Official Eurostat estimates,[237] at the end of the July 2011 show a 23% increase in the work permits applications from immigrants in southern European countries, where economic crisis hit hard and where unemployment varies from the rate of 22% in Spain to the 9.2% in Italy. These figures do not take into account those immigrants working illegally.

Believing that Europe, and especially southern Member States, can easily absorb a new immigration wave that has been fueled by strife and uncertain political outcome is a far-fetched hypothesis and needs to be addressed in a balanced and coherent manner. In 2012 such immigration waves will carry the increasing risk of destabilizing fundamentalist infiltrates amongst peaceful and well-intentioned individuals and families. Social and security distress of the civil population will increase dramatically and will reflect in the upcoming elections across Europe. If multiculturalism in Europe has failed, the chance of it carrying the seeds of future conflicts is ever present. Let this be a warning that should not be discounted in the least.

---

[237] http://epp.eurostat.ec.europa.eu/portal/page/portal/publications/collections/news_releases

Post Scriptum

DURING THE WRITING OF THIS BOOK two major challenges kept occurring—firstly, the constant and abrupt change in the portrait of the Middle East with the potential to generate new faces and names emerging as leaders and politically active players.

Secondly, the nature of the subject is so delicate and controversial that it created intense debate between the two authors themselves, one Gennaro Buonocore representing the more liberal point of view and the other "Christian Von Rosen-Kreutz" representing a more conservative and radical segment of the European population. This confirms that the aim of the book is primarily to stimulate dialogue and create solution through debate. The matter which both the authors wholeheartedly agreed upon was that the multicultural Europe has truly failed and that the causes need to be finally addressed before Europe reaches the point of no return.

With regard to the political changes in the Islamic world, protagonists of the Islamic scene who were described in the book were no longer alive by the time a chapter was completed. However the message of this book does not change, it is actually reinforced by what is being witnessed: a hardening of fundamentalist views to the detriment of Christian minorities in Egypt, a resurgence of Al Qaida affiliates in Yemen, Somalia and the Maghreb, social unrest and political killings in Tunisia and a hardening of the pro-Iranian posture of Iraq in Mesopotamia.

Recent developments point to a radicalization of those countries where vacuum powers are present.

In a globalized world, a struggling neighbor provokes a ripple effect that cannot be contained or marginalized when economic resources are limited.

The Middle East is now rapidly changing and the pace of change is uncontrollable. Europe has even less time to theorize on its ability to relate to the effects of neighboring revolution with exercises in democratic philosophy.

Again, the message that radical Islam is not compatible with Western-style democracy should be a reminder that the potential for greater conflicts is increasing and needs to be met with appropriate action.

Unwillingness to realize the potential disaster will be one of history's greatest blunders.

"Europe is no longer Europe, it is Eurabia, a colony of Islam, where the Islamic invasion does not proceed only in a physical sense, but also in a mental and cultural sense…

Instead of learned young people we have donkeys with University degrees. Instead of future leaders we have mollusks with expensive blue jeans and phony revolutionaries with ski masks. And do you know what? Maybe this is another reason why our Muslim invaders have such an easy game…

The moment you give up your principles, and your values, you are dead, your culture is dead, your civilization is dead. Period. "

— ORIANA FALLACI 1929–2006 AUTHOR OF
THE RAGE AND THE PRIDE, A MAN, LETTER TO A CHILD NEVER BORN, INSHALLAH AND THE FORCE OF REASON

Annex 1—Figures of migration in Europe

IGRANT POPULATION in Europe has reached in 2008 approximately 69 millions, or 9.5%, of which about 34 million— or 52% of total immigrants—are of non-European origin (according to the UN definition of non-European origin), out of a total population of approx. 831 million:[238]

- Arabs (including North African and Middle Eastern Arabs): approx. 18 million, mostly in France, Italy, the Netherlands, Belgium, Germany, United Kingdom, Sweden, Spain, Norway, Denmark, Switzerland, Greece and Russia.

- North African Arabs : approx. 15 million, mostly in France, Italy, the Netherlands, Belgium, Spain and Greece.

- Middle Eastern Arabs: approx. 3 million mostly in United Kingdom, Germany, France, Italy, the Netherlands, Switzerland, Sweden, Denmark, Norway, Greece and Russia.

- Black Africans (including Afro-Caribbeans and others by descent): approx. 6 million; mostly in Italy, France, the

---

[238] Source: United Nations, Trends in Migrant Stock: The 2008 Revision, data in digital form in 2008, see http://esa.un.org/migration/p2k0data.asp.

United Kingdom, Germany, Spain, the Netherlands and Portugal (in Spain and Portugal, Afro-Caribbean and Afro-Latin American are included in Latin Americans).

- Turks (including from Turkey and North Cyprus): approx. 5 million, mostly in Germany, Italy, France, the EU, the Netherlands, Austria and Belgium (see Turks in Europe).

- South Asians: approx. 4 million; mostly in the United Kingdom, Italy, Germany and the Netherlands.

- Pakistanis: approx. 1 million; in the United Kingdom, but also 60,000 in Italy, Spain and Norway.

- Tamils: approx. 250,000 in the United Kingdom, Germany, Italy, Switzerland, Finland, Norway, Sweden and Denmark.

- Latin Americans (includes Afro-Latin Americans, Afro-Caribbean's, Native Americans, White Latin Americans, miscegenation, etc.): approx. 2.2 million; mostly in Spain (1.5 million) but also in Italy, Portugal and the United Kingdom.

- Armenians: approx. 2 million, mostly in France, but also in EU, Germany, Netherlands and Russia.

- Berbers: approx. 2 million, mostly in France, Italy, the Netherlands, Belgium and Spain.

- Kurds: approx. 1.5 million, mostly in Germany, The Netherlands and Sweden,

- Chinese: approx. 1 million; mostly in Italy, France, the United Kingdom, Spain, the Netherlands and Russia.

- Filipinos: approx. 500,000; mostly in the United Kingdom, Italy, Spain and Germany.

- Vietnamese: approx. 300,000; mostly in France, Italy, Germany and Russia.

- Iranians: approx. 250,000; mostly in the United Kingdom, Italy, France, Germany, Spain, Netherlands, Norway, Sweden, Finland and Denmark.

- Horn Africans: approx. 200,000 Somalis mostly in the United Kingdom, Netherlands, Norway, Sweden, Finland and Denmark.

Bibliography

Aradau, Claudia, "Trafficking in Women: Human Rights or Human Risks?" in *Canadian Woman Studies 22(3–4): 55–9*, (2003).

Balibar, Etienne (2004) We, the People of Europe? (Princeton UP).

Berman, Jacqueline (2003) Popular Strangers and Crises Bounded: Discourses of Sex-Trafficking, the European Political Community and the Panicked States of the Modern State in *European Journal of International Relations 9(1): 37–86.*

Bigo (2001) "When Two become One: Internal and External Securitisations in Europe," in Kelstrup, M. And Williams, M. (eds).

Charles Smith, the Arab-Israeli Conflict, in International Relations in the Middle East by Louise Fawcett.

The Crime Conundrum Veyne, Paul (1997) "Foucault revolutionizes history" in A. Davidson (ed.) Foucault and his Interlocutors.

Daily Telegraph. Islam poses a threat to the West, say 53% in poll. 25 August 2006.

De Genova, Nicolas (2002) Migrant "Illegality" and Deportability in Everyday Life in Annual Review of Anthropology 31: 419–471 Foucault, Michel (1997) Discipline and Punish: Birth of the Prison (Penguin).

Hindess, Barry (1998) "Neoliberalism and the National Economy" in Dean and Hindess (eds) Governing Australia Hindess, Barry (2000) "Citizenship in the International Management of Population," *American Behavioral Scientist* 43(9): 1486–97.

Ian Dunt (7 May 2009). "Muslims more patriotic than Brits". *Politics.*

International Relations Theory and the Politics of European Integration (Routledge). CEC (2001) European Governance. A White Paper. COM (2001) 428 final. Brussels 25 July.

Lavenex, Sandra and Uçarer, Emek (2003) The Emergent EU Migration Regime and its External Impact in Lavenex & Uçarer (eds) Migration and the Externalities of European Integration Mann, Michael (199X) Sources of Social Power Volume II (Cambridge University Press).

Pascal Bruckner—Enlightenment fundamentalism or racism of the anti-racists? originally appeared in German in the online magazine *Perlentaucher* on January 24, 2007.

Paul Cliteur, Moderne Papoea's, Dilemma's van een multi-culturele samenleving, De Uitgeverspers, 2002.

Reflections on the Revolution in Europe: Immigration, Islam, and the West. London, Allen Lane, 2009.

Sara Silvestri, Islam and the EU: the merits and risks of Inter-Cultural Dialogue, Policy Brief, European Policy Centre, June 2007.

Simon, Jonathan (1997) "Governing through Crime" in Friedman and Fisher (eds).

Tariq Modood (2006-04-06). *Multiculturalism, Muslims and Citizenship: A European Approach (1st Ed.)*. Routledge. pp. 3, 29, 46.

Vikram Dood (21 October 2006). "White pupils less tolerant, survey shows". *The Guardian*.

Walid Phares, "The Coming Revolution: Struggle for Freedom in the Middle East," Amazon.com books

Walters, William (2002) "Mapping Schengenland: Denaturalizing the Border," Environment and Planning D: Society and Space 20(5): 561–80.

Will Canada introduce Sharia law? BBC News, 26 August 2004.

Z.V. Togan: The Origins of the Kazaks and the Ozbeks, *Central Asian Survey Vol. 11, No. 3*. 1992.

Meforum.org
JHUBC.it
Diis.dk
Ec.europa.eu
Telegraph.co.uk
Dhimmitude.org
Esib.org
Minhajalam.wordpress.com
Islamicsupremecouncil.org
Cedarsrevolution.net
Ivestigativeproject.org
Eesc.europa.eu
Claremont.org

turkishweekly.net
NYTimes.org
Medilibrary.org
Iht.com
Irr.org.uk
Bnp.org.uk
Euraction.org
Colgate.edu
Epp.eurostat.ec.europa.eu
Transnationalterrorism.eu
Mcb.org.uk
Libertysecurity.org
Islam-watch.org

CPSIA information can be obtained at www.ICGtesting.com
Printed in the USA
LVOW060856030612

284398LV00003B/2/P